Short C
Walks
Staffor
Moorlands

by

John N. Merrill

Maps and photographs by John N. Merrill

The Short Circular Walks Series

2000

Produced by a member of THE GUILD OF MASTER CRAFTSMEN

Happy Walking International Ltd

Happy Walking International Ltd.,
Unit 1, Molyneux Business Park,
Whitworth Road, Darley Dale,
Matlock, Derbyshire, England.
DE4 2HJ

Tel/Fax 01629 - 735911
Email - John.Merrill@virgin.net
www.happywalkinginternational.co.uk

Printed, bound, marketed and distributed by Happy Walking International Ltd.

ISBN 0 907496 40 7 First published - October 1986
Reprinted - September 1999

British Library Cataloguing-in-Publication Data. A catalogue record of this book is available from the British Library.

Typeset in Bookman MS bold, italic, and plain 10pt, 14pt and 18pt,

Please note - The maps in this guide are purely illustrative. You are encouraged to use the appropriate 1:25,000 O.S. map.

Meticulous research has been undertaken to ensure that this publication is highly accurate at the time of going to press. The publishers, however, cannot be held responsible for alterations, errors, omissions, or for changes in details given. They would welcome information to

CONTENTS

ABOUT JOHN N. MERRILL

Few people have walked the earth's crust more than John Merrill with more than 168,000 miles in the last 28 years -the average person walks 75,000 miles in a lifetime. Apart from walking too much causing bones in his feet to snap, like metal fatigue, he has never suffered from any back, hip or knee problems. Like other walkers he has suffered from many blisters, his record is 23 on both feet! He wears out at least three pairs of boots a year and his major walking has cost over £125,000. This includes 87 pairs of boots costing more than £10,200 and over £1,200 on socks - a pair of socks last three weeks and are not washed.

His marathon walks in Britain include - -

Hebridean Journey....... 1,003 miles. Northern Isles Journey......913 miles.
Irish Island Journey ....1,578 miles. Parkland Journey.......2,043 miles.
Land's End to John o' Groats.....1,608 miles.

and in 1978 he became the first person to walk the entire coastline of Britain - 6,824 miles in ten months.

In Europe he has walked across Austria - 712 miles - hiked the Tour of Mont Blanc, the Normandy coast, the Loire Valley (450 miles), a high level route across the Augverne(230 miles) and the River Seine (200 miles) in France, completed High Level Routes in the Dolomites and Italian Alps, and the GR20 route across Corsica in training! Climbed the Tatra Mountains ,the Transylvanian Alps in Romania, and in Germany walked in the Taunus, Rhine, the Black Forest (Clock Carriers Way) and King Ludwig Way (Bavaria). He has walked across Europe - 2,806 miles in 107 days - crossing seven countries, the Swiss and French Alps and the complete Pyrennean chain - the hardest and longest mountain walk in Europe, with more than 600,000 feet of ascent! In 1998 he walked 1,100 miles along the pilgrimage route from Le Puy (France) to Santiago (Spain) and onto Cape Finisterre.

In America he used The Appalachian Trail - 2,200 miles - as a training walk, before walking from Mexico to Canada via the Pacific Crest Trail in record time - 118 days for 2,700 miles. Recently he walked most of the Continental Divide Trail and much of New Mexico; his second home. In 1999 he walked the Chesopeake & Ohio Canal National Historical Trail. In Canada he has walked the Rideau Trail - Kingston to Ottowa - 220 miles and The Bruce Trail - Tobermory to Niagara Falls - 460 miles.

In 1984 John set off from Virginia Beach on the Atlantic coast, and walked 4,226 miles without a rest day, across the width of America to Santa Cruz and San Francisco on the Pacific coast. His walk is unquestionably his greatest achievement, being, in modern history, the longest, hardest crossing of the U.S.A. in the shortest time - under six months (178 days). The direct distance is 2,800 miles.

Between major walks John is out training in his own area - The Peak District National Park. He has walked all of our National Trails many times - The Cleveland Way thirteen times and The Pennine Way four times in a year! He has been trekking in the Himalayas five times. He created more than thirty-five challenge walks which have been used to raise more than £600,000 for charity. From his own walks he has raised over £100,000. He is author of more than 180 walking guides which he prints and publishes himself, His book sales are in excess of 3 million, He has created many long distance walks including The Limey Way , The Peakland Way, Dark Peak Challenge walk, Rivers' Way, The Belvoir Witches Challenge Walk and the Forest of Bowland Challenge.

INTRODUCTION

Lying on the south-western side of the Peak District National Park is some of England's finest walking countryside. The incomparable beauty of Dovedale is well known, together with its northern dales of Wolfscote and Beresford. The river Dove that flows through them is the county boundary of Derbyshire and Staffordshire. A little further west is the Manifold Valley, more open than the Dove but equally scenic and rich in history. Further west and now outside the National Park, is the Churnet Valley. The walking here is equally as good, with the picturesque village of Alton often referred to as the 'Rhineland' because of its castle and neighbouring Tower. Not only are there good dales and forests to explore but a major section of the Caldon Canal can be followed and traced.

I have endeavoured to encompass all the variety of the area into the walks in this book. Some pass through the popular areas but many are in quiet areas, on defined paths. Walks such as over to Bradley in the Moors or to Denstone are particularly enjoyable. I have included a handful of walks partly in Derbyshire to illustrate and attempt to complete the walking scene. The Osmaston walk is a firm favourite of mine and I first walked it twenty years ago! Mayfield is another full of interest with its Hanging Bridge and Okeover Hall. The short ascent of the Weaver Hills gives you a panoramic view over the walking area and serves as a curtain raiser to your walking exploration.

Here then is a comprehensive selection of walks in some of the finest scenery imaginable. I derive tremendous pleasure from exploring the area and discovering new paths through well known areas seeing items from different view points. I hope you too enjoy these various walks and, like me continue to return whatever the season and walk them in winter or summer.

Happy walking!
John N. Merrill

ABOUT THE WALKS

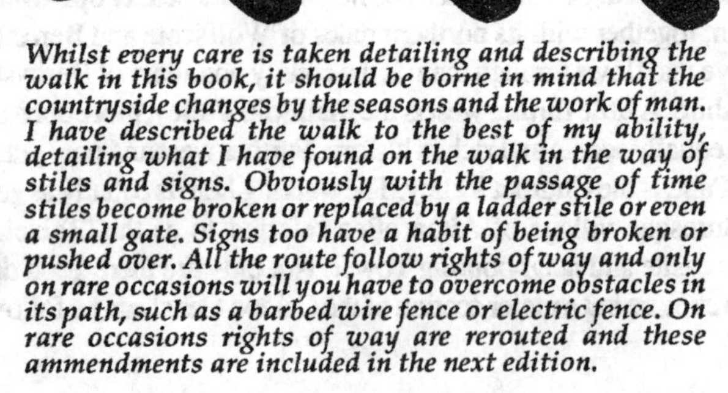

Whilst every care is taken detailing and describing the walk in this book, it should be borne in mind that the countryside changes by the seasons and the work of man. I have described the walk to the best of my ability, detailing what I have found on the walk in the way of stiles and signs. Obviously with the passage of time stiles become broken or replaced by a ladder stile or even a small gate. Signs too have a habit of being broken or pushed over. All the route follow rights of way and only on rare occasions will you have to overcome obstacles in its path, such as a barbed wire fence or electric fence. On rare occasions rights of way are rerouted and these ammendments are included in the next edition.

The seasons bring occasional problems whilst out walking which should also be borne in mind. In the height of summer paths become overgrown and you will have to fight your way through in a few places. In low lying areas the fields are often full of crops, and although the pathline goes straight across it may be more practical to walk round the field edge to get to the next stile or gate. In summer the ground is generally dry but in autumn and winter, especially because of our climate, the surface can be decidedly wet and slippery; sometimes even gluttonous mud!

These comments are part of countryside walking which help to make your walk more interesting or briefly frustrating. Standing in a farmyard up to your ankles in mud might not be funny at the time but upon reflection was one of the highlights of the walk!

The mileage for each walk is based on three calculations -

1. pedometer reading.
2. the route map measured on the map.
3. the time I took for the walk.

I believe the figure stated for each walk to be very accurate but we all walk differently and not always in a straight line! The time allowed for each walk is on the generous side and does not include pub stops etc. The figure is based on the fact that on average a person walks 2 1/2 miles an hours but less in hilly terrain.

Milldale.

The Caldon Canal.

ASHBOURNE AND THE TISSINGTON TRAIL—6 miles

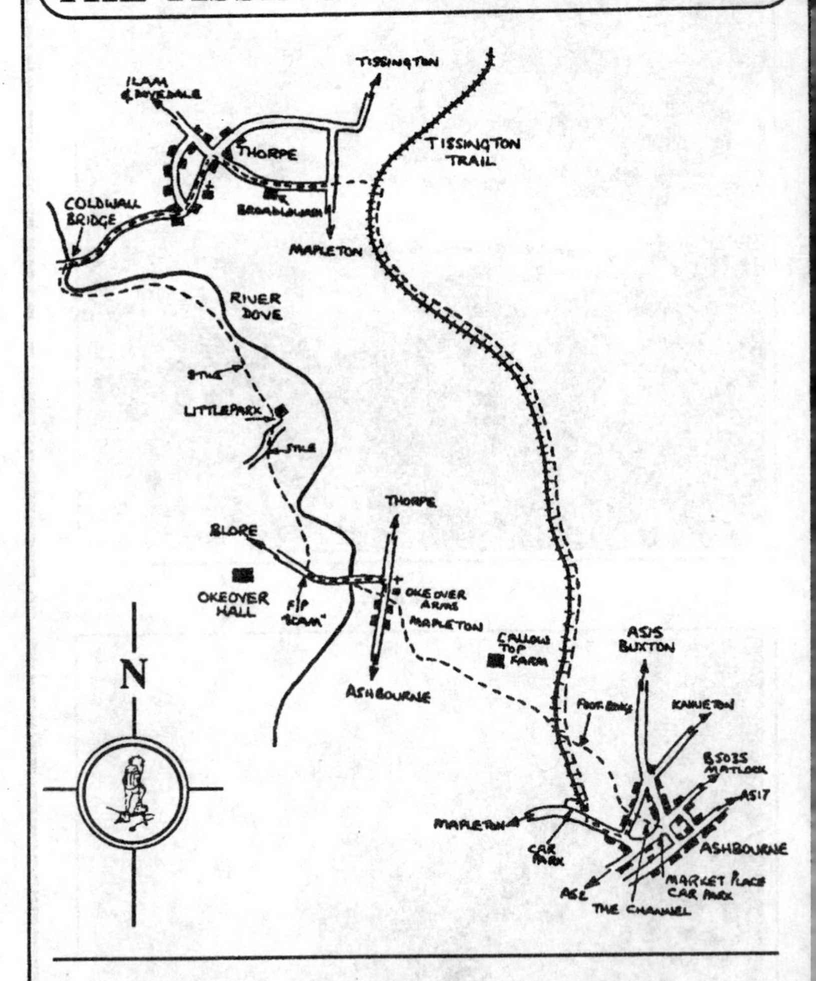

TISSINGTON TRAIL—former Ashbourne to Buxton railway line, converted to pedestrian, cycleway and bridleway in 1971. 13 miles are open to the public, from Ashbourne to Parsley Hay.

ASHBOURNE—a market town well worth exploring, containing many historical buildings—Church Street is one of the finest 17th century streets in England. The church dedicated to St. Oswald is often referred to as 'The Pride of the Peak'. The spire is 215 feet high and weighs 300 tons. The Shrovetide football game held each year is unique and between the Up'ards and Down'ards, depending on what side of the Henmore Brook you were born on.

ASHBOURNE AND THE TISSINGTON TRAIL—6 miles

—allow 2 1/2 hours

—1:25,000 Outdoor Leisure Map—The White Peak—East Sheet
1:25,000 Pathfinder Sheet SK 04/14—Ashbourne and the Churnet Valley

—Ashbourne Market Place

ABOUT THE WALK—From Ashbourne you first cross the fields to the Tissington Trail before reaching the village of Mapleton. From here you cross the River Dove and enter Staffordshire and walk along the river banks to Coldwall Bridge. A short ascent brings you to Thorpe and its attractive village. You return to Ashbourne along the Tissington Trail.

WALKING INSTRUCTIONS—From the Market Place walk up the 'Channel' on the immediate right of the public conveniences. At the top of this cobbled path cross the road and follow the path signposted—Dovedale. Once clear of the houses you bear right using stiles and descend the fields to the footbridge across Bradbourne Brook. Bear right to the Tissington Trail and cross it and ascend the field to a stile. Beyond, it levels out as you keep the field hedge on your right and head for Mapleton. Over the brow of the hill you can see the small village, and after descending a short distance you bear right to the village walking between the houses close to the Okeover Arms Inn.

Turn right then left through the stile and cross the field to the Dove bridge. On your right is Mapleton Church. Cross the bridge over the River Dove, and almost opposite the entrance gates to Okeover Hall turn right following the signposted path to Ilam. For the next 1/4 mile you walk near the banks of the river, but after a wooden stile you cross a field to the farm track to the left of Littlepark. Turn right to the farm and just before the buildings bear left and cross the field beyond, passing the prominent remains of a dead oak tree. Just after you descend to a wood and the River Dove. The next mile near the river to Coldwall Bridge is well defined and stiled.

At the bridge turn right along it and ascend the track to Thorpe village 1/2 mile away. Walk past the church and turn right up the winding lane past Broadlowash to a T junction. Here keep straight ahead to the Tissington Trail 200 yards away. Turn right and follow the trail for 2 miles. In the final stages you will walk over the Bradbourne Brook to gain the car park beside the tunnel. Here turn right then left and ascend the road. At the top turn left then right into the 'Channel' and descend back to the Market Place.

MAYFIELD - 5 MILES

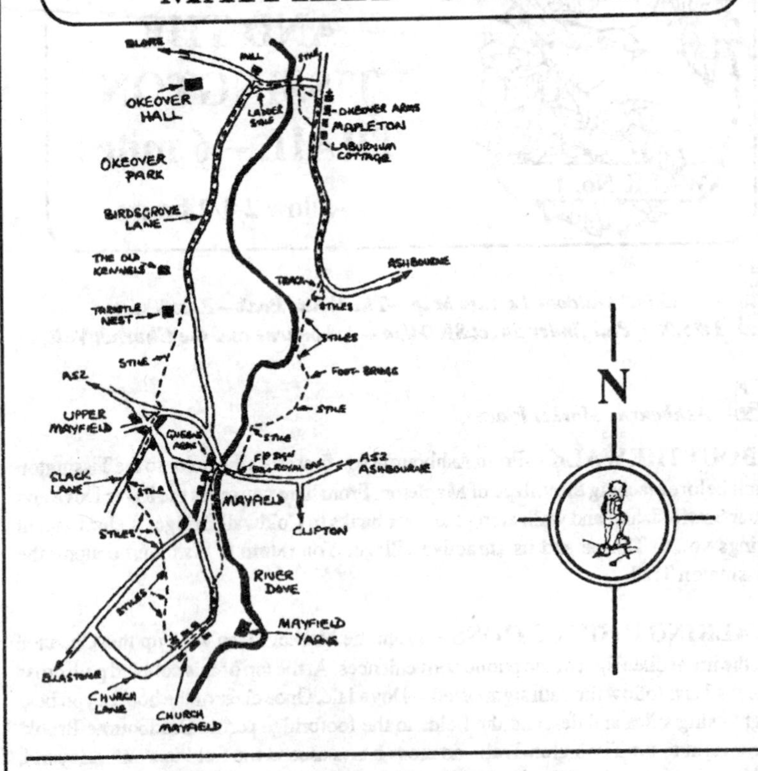

- from opposite page -

the path to the A52 road beside the Royal Oak Inn. Turn right over the bridge and left onto the Mayfield road. 50 yards later, as footpath signed turn left and descend to the river Dove. Keep beside it for just over 1/4 mile to the ascending steps. Ascend these to the stile and cross the football field to a stile beside the gate. Turn left along the road, passing the entrance to Mayfield Yarns and regain Church Mayfield.

CHURCH MAYFIELD—the Church dedicated to St. John the Baptist, dates from Norman times. The chancel has Jacobean carvings and the communion rail was carved in 1660. The tower was built in 1515 by Thomas Rolleston; the French inscription on the outside means—*'So it is, and better could it be!'*

OKEOVER HALL—the present Palladian styled building was built between 1701-1765 by Leake Okeover. The wrought iron entrance gates were made by Robert Bakewell in the 18th century.

HANGING BRIDGE, MAYFIELD—the modern single arched bridge covers the mediaeval two arched packhorse bridge. The road is Roman in origin, known as Hereward Street, and linked the Roman forts of Rochester and Chesterfield together.

MAYFIELD —5 MILES

—allow 2 1/2 hours

O.S. MAP —*1:25,000 Pathfinder Sheet SK 04/14—Ashbourne and the Churnet Valley*

P —*no official one at Mapleton or Mayfield.*

ABOUT THE WALK—I have started the walk from the southern end at Church Mayfield, whose church is particularly attractive and full of interest. From here you cross fields to Upper Mayfield before entering Okeover Park and see Okeover Hall. Up to now you have been in Staffordshire but on crossing the River Dove you enter Derbyshire. First you have the option of exploring Mapleton Church before walking close to the river to Hanging bridge and seeing the present bridge over the earlier one. Back in Staffordshire you continue beside the river to regain Church Mayfield. There are three inns on this walk!

WALKING INSTRUCTIONS—Walk through the churchyard to the church, dedicated to St.John the Baptist, and turn right along the path to the gate—now heading due north. The path is well defined across the fields and well stiled. Continue past the houses on your right to the road—B5032. Cross over to stile and gently ascend to the top lefthand corner and stile. Go diagonally across two more fields before keeping the field boundary on your left to reach Slack Lane. Walk up the lane and at the top turn left then right and descend to the A52 road. Turn right then left almost immediately onto a descending track to a gate and stile. Over this continue ahead keeping to the right of a barn, keeping the field boundary on your right. Two more stiles beside gates bring you to the track close to Throstle Nest. Cross the field to a gate on your right and reach Birdsgrove Lane. Turn left along this and enter Okeover Park. Keep on the road for almost a mile to the road junction opposite a mill. Turn right over the River Dove Bridge and enter Derbyshire.

Turn right at the stile beside the path sign and cross the field to Mapleton, opposite the Okeover Arms. Turn right and follow the road, heading southwards, for 3/4 mile. Where the road turns left and begins to climb with a wood ahead, turn right and descend a track to gate and stile. Bear right and cross the field to a stile close to the River Dove. Walk beside the Dove to the end of the field, and over the stile turn left beside the field boundary to a footbridge over Bentley Brook. Turn right and keep the brook on your right to the next stile, then a gate and close to the earth embankment. Keep close to this to the next stile close to the River Dove. Turn left over another stile and walk along

- continued opposite -

OSMASTON - 4 1/2 MILES

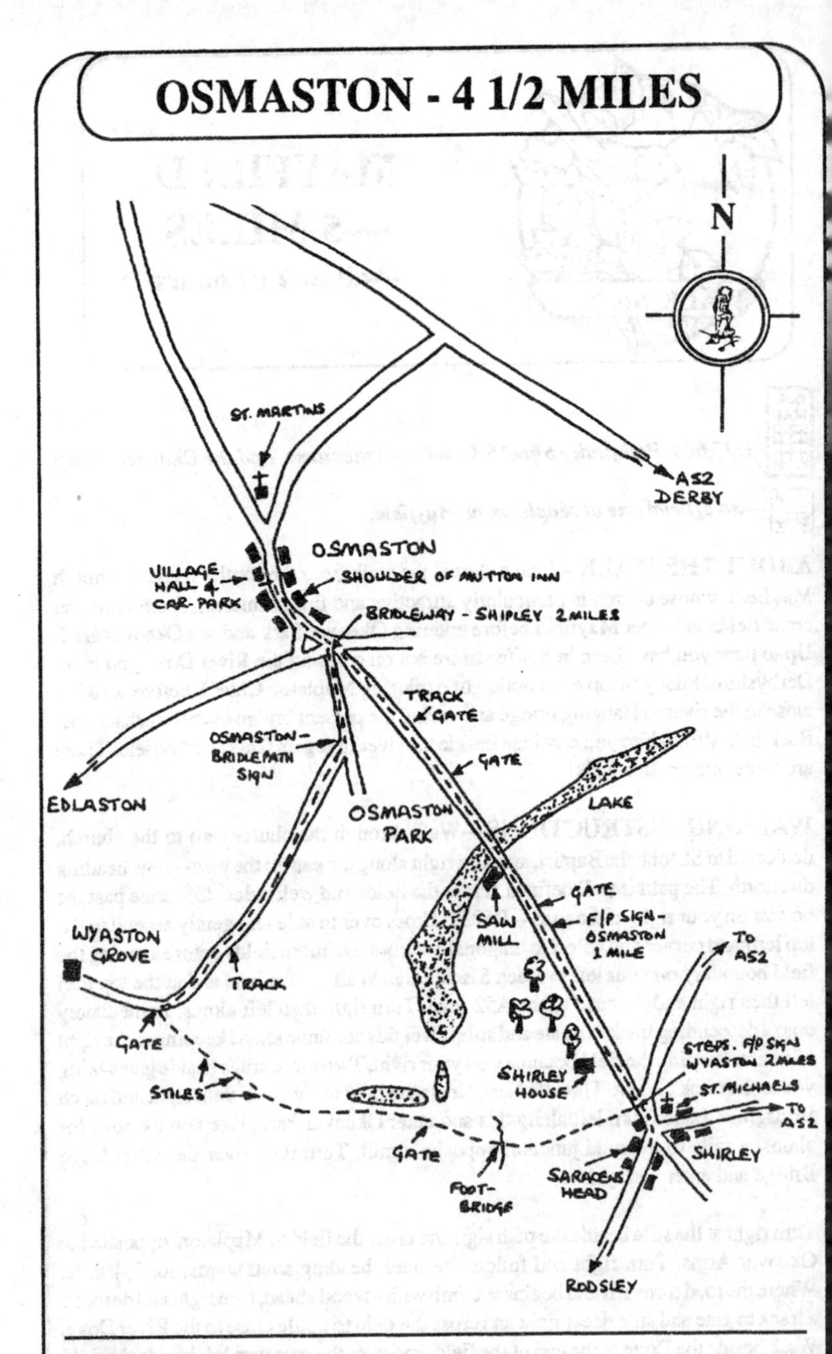

OSMASTON—beautiful model thatched village. Osmaston Manor has now been demolished but was built in 1865 and was perfectly sited overlooking lakes and woodland.

OSMASTON —4 1/2 MILES

—allow 2 1/2 hours

1:25,000 Pathfinder Sheet No SK 04/14—Ashbourne and the Churnet Valley
—1:25,000 Pathfinder Sheet No SK 24/34—Belper

—beside Village Hall in Osmaston.

ABOUT THE WALK—Osmaston is a particularly attractive village with numerous thatched houses. You cross and encircle Osmaston Park, once the location of an impressive house; now demolished. The parkland remains with lakes, a water driven saw mill and elegant cedar trees. At Shirley, apart from an inn there is an interesting church to explore. An ideal walk for all the family!

WALKING INSTRUCTIONS—Turn right out of the car park through Osmaston, passing the Shoulder of Mutton Inn on your left and several thatched houses. At the pond bear left to the path sign at the entrance to Osmaston Park. The Wyaston bridleway through the entrance is your return path. Take the track on your left, signed—Bridlepath to Shirley, 2 miles. The track is basically straight all the way to Shirley—ignore all cross paths. Pass through a small wood and descend to the lakes and sawmill. Continue ahead climbing, still on a track, and walk beside Shirley Park Wood on your right. 1/2 mile later leave the park and follow the now tarmaced lane to Shirley. At the road junction on your right is the path sign—Wyaston and steps. Before ascending these continue ahead into Shirley to see its church and yew tree and the inn, The Saracens Head.

Return to the road junction and ascend the steps and follow the fenced path to the stile. Cross it and follow the field boundary on your left to the next wooden stile.Here keep the field boundary on your right to the next stile. Cross the following field to another stile and descend to a footbridge over Shirley Brook. Bear right beside the wood to a wooden gate. Here enter the woodland following a defined path/track through the pine trees. After 1/4 mile reach another gate with Fish Lake just beyond. Follow the path along its lefthand side before walking close to a strip of woodland on your right for 1/4 mile. The path is well stiled. Where there is a break in the woodland with curving fence to a gate, turn right through the gate and follow the track back into Osmaston Park. Ascend past a house and as bridlepath signed turn left, at the drive and at the next road junction left again to the entrance gate and pond you passed at the beginning. Turn left and retrace your steps back to the village hall car park.

CALWICH ABBEY AND RIVER DOVE - 4 1/2 MILES

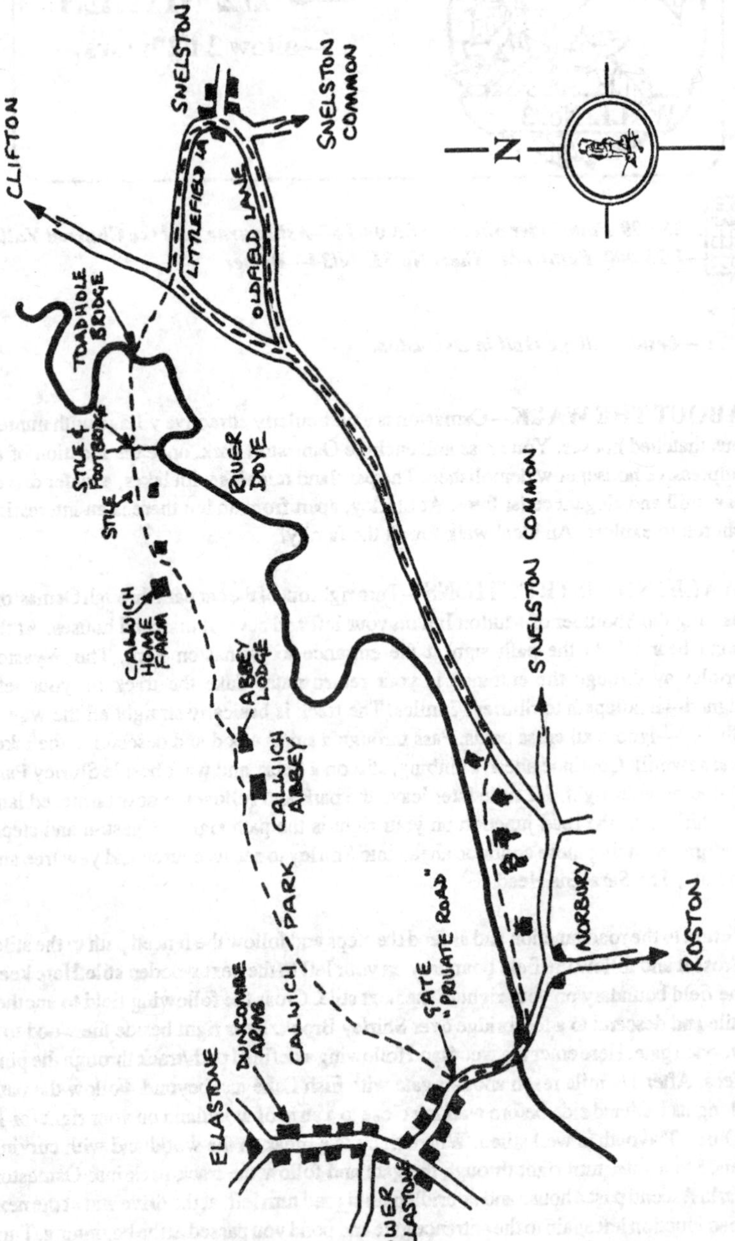

CALWICH ABBEY AND RIVER DOVE —4 1/2 MILES

—allow 2 hours

O.S. MAP *—1:25,000 Pathfinder Sheet No SK 04/14 —Ashbourne and the Churnet Valley*

P *—no official car park.*

ABOUT THE WALK—a very pleasant walk up the Dove valley, through Calwich Park and impressive mansion to the Toadhole footbridge over the Dove. Upon reaching the road a 3/4 mile extension will bring you into the attractive village of Snelston. The final part of the walk is beside the Dove and through pine forest. A visit to Norbury Church is particularly interesting to see the Fitzherberts' memorials and hall.

WALKING INSTRUCTIONS—Starting from the road bridge over the River Dove, midway between Norbury and Ellastone, follow the road towards Lower Ellastone. Just where you enter, turn right to a gate and drive—Private Road. This is the footpath through Calwich Park. The drive is well fenced. Simply keep ahead to the next gate where you enter open country. 1/2 mile later gain the gate with the impressive stable block of Calwich Abbey beyond. Follow the track first to your left then right past Abbey Lodge. Continue on the drive over the cattle grid to the next one, 1/2 mile later, close to Calwich Home Farm. Cross another shortly afterwards and turn right down the track. Where it enters a private house descend to your left to a stile and pass the rock escarpment to the river plain and a stile and footbridge. Cross the next field to the River Dove and prominent Toadhole Foot Bridge. Follow the stiled track beyond to the road. You now follow the road to your right for 3/4 mile, but by crossing over and following—Littlefield Lane— you can explore the village of Snelston. In the village turn right, then right again onto—Oldfield Lane—and this will return you to the Norbury road.

At the road turn right and follow it for 3/4 mile. Pass a couple of cottages on your right and Norbury sign on your left. 30 yards later turn right into the pine trees and follow the path above the river for 1/2 mile to a stile and footbridge over a mill leat, with a weir on your right. Ascend another stile beyond before following the banks of the Dove to your right to the road bridge where you started. To visit Norbury Church instead of walking through the pine trees, continue on the road, turning right at all junctions. The church is signed on your right.

WEAVER HILLS - 3 MILES

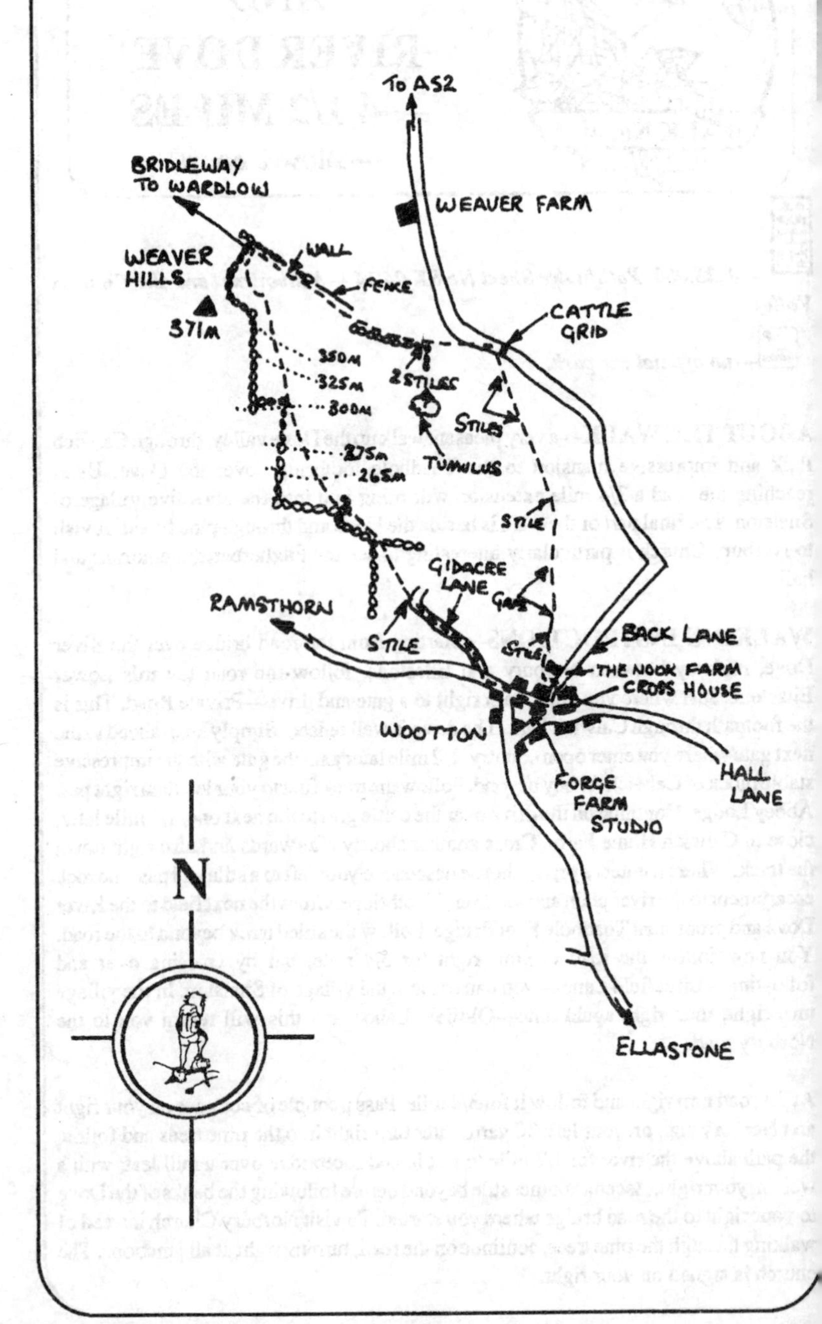

WEAVER HILLS — 3 MILES

—allow 1 1/2 hours

1:25,000 Pathfinder Sheet No SK 04/14—Ashbourne and the Churnet Valley.

—no official one in Wootton.

ABOUT THE WALK—The Weaver Hills provide an extensive and stunning vantage point of the Churnet Valley, Staffordshire, southern Derbyshire and southern Peakland. The view is 360 degrees. There is parking on the road— signposted in Wootton, Weaver Hills—but to me that is cheating getting there by car! This walk provides an easy ascent to the summit with an enjoyable descent. When you get there you have earned the view!

WALKING INSTRUCTIONS—Start the walk in the centre of Wootton, near Cross House and Forge Farm Studio. The road on your right—Back Lane signposted for the Weaver Hills—is the final part of your return route. Walk to the main road—Ellastone/Ramsthorn road, and continue ahead towards Ramsthorn. 30 yards later and just past the farm on your right, is the hedged track, known as Gidacre Lane. Follow this as it bears left, gently ascending. Where it turns sharp right, continue to a wooden stile. Cross the field beyond, bearing right slightly as you ascend to the top lefthand corner of the field. In the next field bear left slightly, still ascending to the fence and stile. Over this continue ascending, bearing slightly right to the top lefthand corner; a little to the right is the stile. The path line is not discernible on the ground, but the route is obvious. Over this wall and fence you begin ascending more steeply, keeping the wall well to your left at first, with a shallow saddle beyond. Ascend a fence—which has been cut out—and bear left towards the wall. All the time you have been ascending, the trig point on the summit of the Weaver Hills has acted as a useful landmark. Your line has been well to the right of it. Keep the wall on your left and over the brow of the summit plateau reach the wall and track. Here you join the bridleway to Wardlow.

Turn right and follow the track first beside the wall, then fence to a gate. The wall is now on your right and in the next field gain a double stile by the gate. Keep straight ahead with the fence on your right to the road. All the time the prominent tumulus with solitary tree on top, on your right, has been a field away.Follow the road to the cattle grid. Don't cross it—turn right to the stile and begin the descent to Wootton. Keep the wall on your left to the next stile. The stiles now guide you down, and at the third stile keep the hedge on your left. Keep straight ahead through two field gaps before gaining the stile before the farm track of Nook Farm on your left. Cross the track to the next stile and descend the field to the stile and path sign by the road—Back Lane. Turn right to reach central Wootton, where you began.

CHEDDLETON & THE CALDON CANAL - 2, 2 1/2, 4 1/2, and 7 miles.

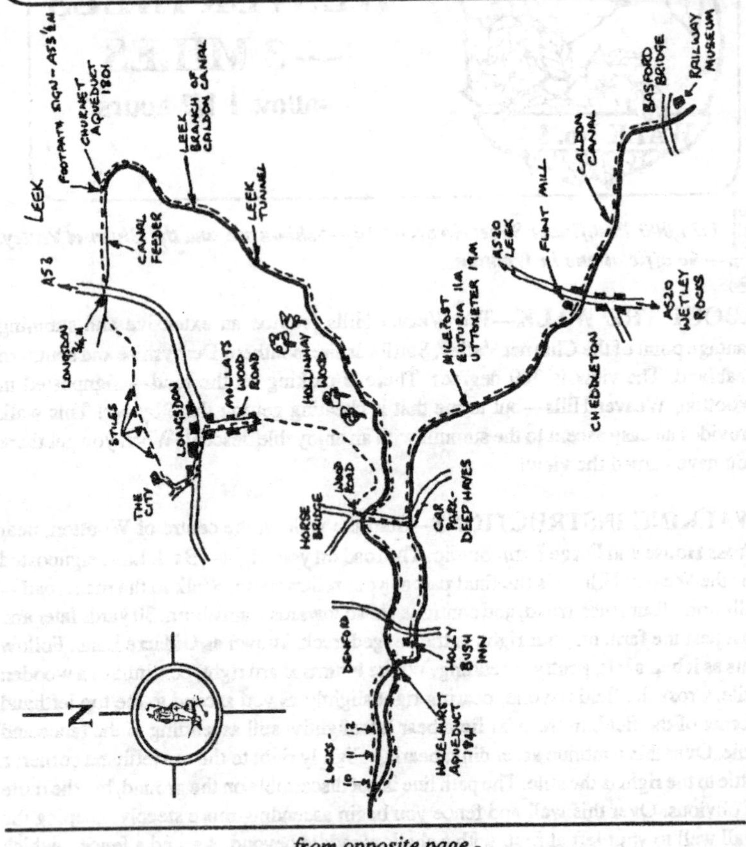

- from opposite page -

as The City, walking round its lefthand edge. Keep left at all road junctions to reach the A53 road. Turn left along the road and about 130 yards later turn right into Mollats Wood Road . Keep straight ahead at all junctions and pass the houses as the road deteriorates into a track as you descend past bracken and woodland. Upon reaching a road (Wood Road), follow it round to your right past the houses to the minor road in Horse Bridge. Turn left along Sutherland Road and cross over the canal and retrace your steps back to the car park.

WALK 4—7 miles. This is walks 2 and 3 joined together.

CHEDDLETON—the flint mills date back to the 17th century and have been restored. Flint was brought here on the adjoining canal and was particularly important material for the pottery industry at nearby Stoke on Trent. The mill machinery can be seen operating most weekends.

CHEDDLETON & THE CALDON CANAL - 2, 2 1/2, 4 1/2 and 7 miles

— allow I to 3 hours

1:25,000 Outdoor Leisure Map—The White Peak (West Sheet)

—Deep Hayes—Grid Ref SJ963534—opposite Horse Bridge.

ABOUT THE WALK—The Caldon Canal is a fascinating place to explore, and particularly so through such a picturesque area. There are several walk options described here of varying lengths, and all hinge on the canal. Firstly there is the Froghall branch to Cheddleton and its amazing flint mill. Secondly there is the Leek branch which uses a section of the Staffordshire Way for your return. Being a figure of eight there are three walk options.

WALKING INSTRUCTIONS—

WALK 1—2 miles—From the car park descend to the canal and turn right along it to Cheddleton to see its Flint Mill. Return the same way. The walk can be extended to continue along the canal to Basford Bridge, 1/2 mile away, to visit the Cheddleton Railway Museum.

WALK 2—2 1/2 miles—From the car park descend to the canal and turn left along it past the Holly Bush Inn at Denford, and under Denford Aqueduct to lock 10 and the junction of the Leek branch. Cross over the metal bridge and follow the Leek branch for a little over a mile to Horse Bridge. Here leave the canal and follow the road to your right over the Froghall branch back to the car park.

WALK 3—4 1/2 miles—From the car park descend to the canal and follow the road to Horse Bridge. Turn right and follow the Leek branch of the Caldon Canal for a little over 2 miles. First pass through Hollinhay Wood before reaching the Leek Tunnel, reopened on April 3rd 1985. A path ascends over the hillside and rejoins the canal which you follow to the outskirts of Leek at the Churnet Aqueduct. Turn left as path signed—A53 1/2 mile. Basically you follow the canal feeder to the road. At the road you join the Staffordshire Way, waymarked with Staffordshire Knots. Cross the road as signed—Longsdon 3/4 mile—and after 20 yards just after a stile turn left and follow the curving path beside the field boundary on your left. Gradually ascend to a stile and enter Longsdon Wood. Continue through it on a well stiled path to the house known

- continued opposite -

FROGHALL AND THE CALDON CANAL - 5 & 6 MILES

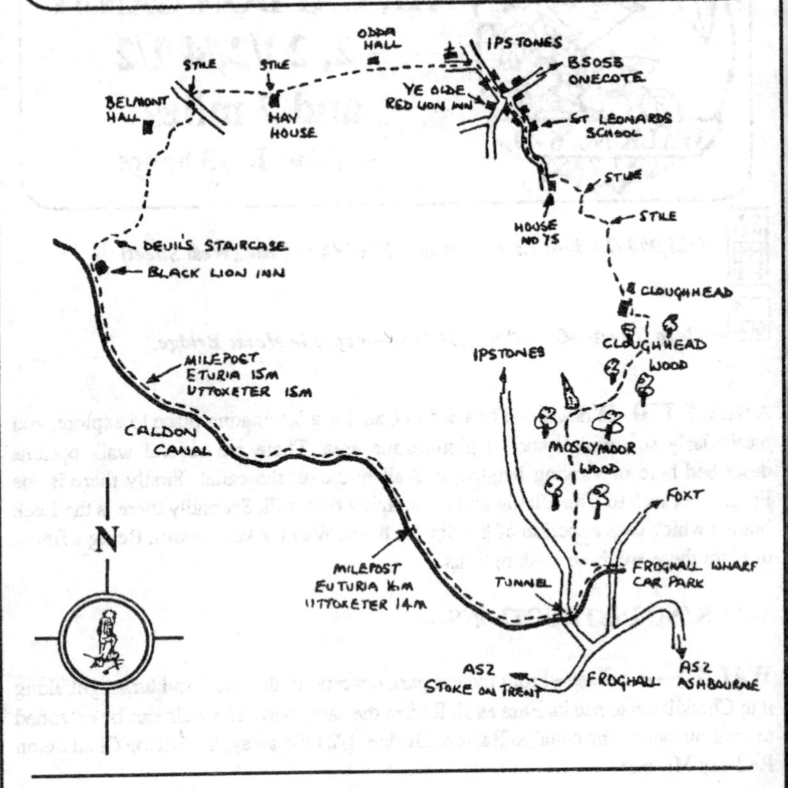

- from opposite page -

the field boundary on your right to the next stile. Here turn right, now heading southwards gently descending to Cloughhead Farm. Pass through the gate to the track and just ahead on your left is the stile. Descend the field to the wood and bear right to the field's bottom righthand corner. The stile is not here but ascend over the wall by the wooden barrier on your right and descend the path in the trees to the footbridge below. Don't cross the bridge but keep on the well used path first beside the stream, then past a small lake on your right before swinging left through Moseymoor Wood back to the Caldon Canal and where you started.

CALDON CANAL—primarily a branch of the Trent & Mersey Canal built in 1779 and is 17 miles long from Froghall to Hanley. Primarily used to carry limestone from Froghall. A branch from Hazelhurst was built in 1797 to Leek. Both these are navigable but the section from Froghall to Uttoxeter built in 1811 has almost disappeared but fragments can still be traced. The Caldon and Leek branch are today one of the loveliest canals in England. The area around Consall Forge is some of the remotest and unspoilt in the country.

FROGHALL AND CALDON CANAL —5 & 6 MILES

—allow 2 1/2 hours

1:25,000 Sheet No SK 04/14—Ashbourne & the Churnet Valley.

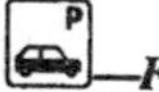

—Froghall Wharf

ABOUT THE WALK—The walk offers two different types of walking, with the Caldon Canal as the central theme. The first walk of 5 miles is simply along the canal to the Black Lion Inn at Consall Forge, whose remoteness and setting is quite unequalled. You return back along the canal, after 'walking for lunch.' The longer walk of 6 miles ascends out of the valley to Ipstones before descending through very attractive woodland back to Froghall.

WALKING INSTRUCTIONS—From Froghall wharf follow the canal westwards to the tunnel, which you walk round, and continue beside the canal for the next 2 1/2 miles to the Black Lion Inn. Here the shorter walk retraces its steps beside the canal back to Froghall. For the longer walk pass in front of the Inn and turn right on the path, which immediately bears left past the out buildings and into woodland. The map refers to the area as the Devil's Staircase, and you will certainly ascend hundreds of concrete steps to the top of the valley. The path is well used as you walk just inside the wood with a wall on your left, with Belmont Hall ahead. Upon reaching the Hall's drive continue ahead along it for 40 yards to a stile and steps on your right. Turn right and descend and cross the footbridge and ascend to road beside path sign—'Consall Forge 3/4 mile, Consall 2 miles.' Turn left past Chapel House and a few yards later right at the stile by the gate. This path is little used. First keep beside the field boundary for 30 yards before bearing right and ascending the field. Cross two fields and aim for the lefthand side of Hay House, where there is a stile. Cross to the next one on the right of the gate and continue across the field to another, keeping the wall on your right. Shortly afterwards you gain a walled track, passing Odda Hall on your left and trig point—273 metres—on your right. Follow the track towards Ipstones, whose church tower has been a useful guideline.

Turn right along the road past the church and down to the B5053 road. Cross over into Brookfields Road, with the Old Red Lion Inn on the opposite side of the road. Descend the road past St.Leonards School and at House No 75 turn left down beside it to a track and follow this past a barn on your right. Turn right just after over a stile and keep the field hedge on your left. Just before the end of the field turn left at the stile and keep

- Continued opposite -

ALTON AND THE CHURNET VALLEY - 5 MILES

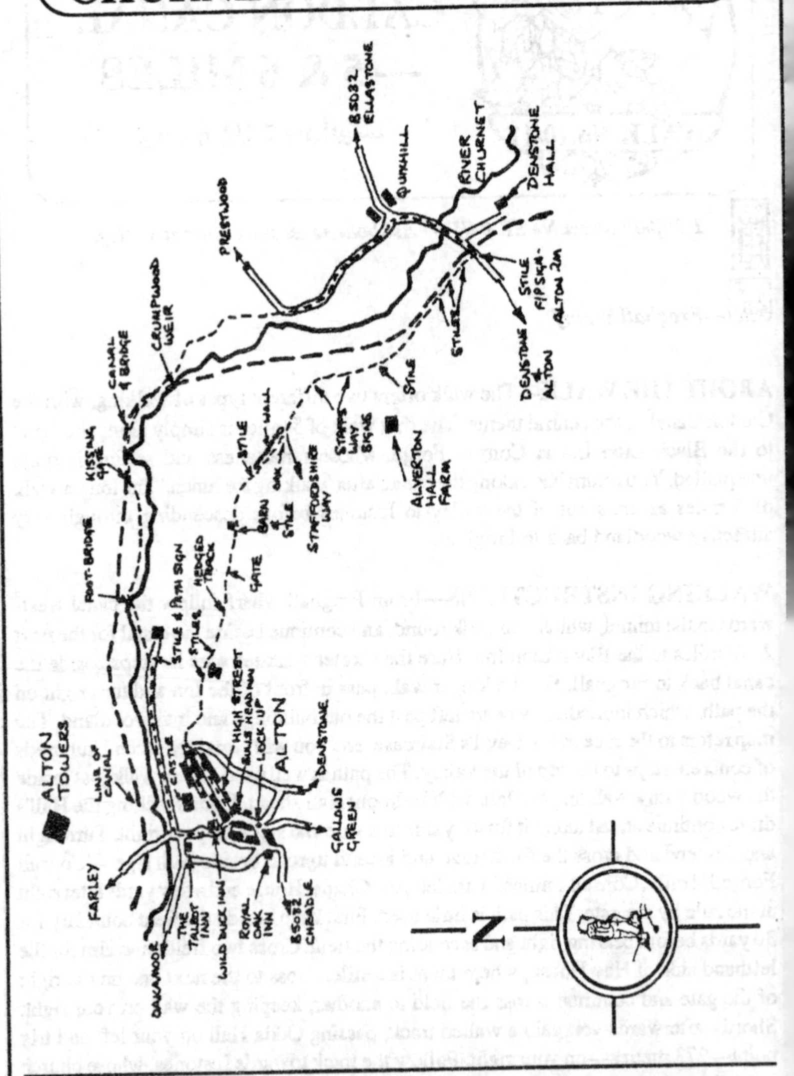

- from opposite page -

brings you to a stone barn. The stile is on the other side of it. Continue ahead across the field before walking beside a hedge on your left to a gate. Here you reach a fenced track which you follow for 1/2 mile to Alton, on the way passing a house and pond on your left. On reaching Alton, you can either keep ahead on Castle Hill passing the castle and descending Church Bank to the Wild Duck Inn, or bear left along Town Head and into the High Street.

ALTON AND THE CHURNET VALLEY — 5 MILES

—allow 2 1/2 hours

— 1:25,000 Sheet No SK 04/14—Ashbourne and the Churnet Valley.

*—No official one in Alton.*

ABOUT THE WALK—Alton is a particularly attractive village and well worth exploring to see the Lock-up, Church, High Street and impressive castle. This walk encircles the village and valley and follows a fragment of the now abandoned Uttoxeter canal. On the walk you can fully appreciate the magnificent setting of the castle and valley.

WALKING INSTRUCTIONS—Starting from the High Street, descend the New Road, northwards to the River Churnet, passing the Wild Duck Inn on your right. Just before the river and almost opposite the branch road on your left— Red Road and the Talbot Inn—turn right onto the track which runs underneath the castle. For the next 1/2 mile keep on this through woodland and the river on your left. Nearing a private house pass through the stile on your left, as path signed, and continue ahead descending gently to the footbridge over the river. Cross the bridge and turn right keeping to the middle of the field, with the river on your right and disused railway line on your left, for a little over 1/4 mile. Pass a metal footbridge over the river before gaining a kissing gate on your left, and cross the railway line. You now walk beside the remains of the Uttoxeter Canal to a splendid canal bridge, with the Crumpwood Switching Station close by. Here you join a tarmaced road and follow it to the impressive Crumpwood Weir. Keep on the road/track for another 1/4 mile before turning right on the track to gain Quixhill Lane. Follow this for 1/2 mile to Quixhill.

Turn right at the road, B5032, and follow it over the river and past Denstone Hall, well to your left. Just after the road turning on your left continue over the railway bridge and as signposted—Alton 2 miles—leave the road and follow the well defined path. Now part of the Staffordshire Way. The path is well stiled and signed as you keep to the righthand edge of the fields. After 1/4 mile you begin to ascend with the remains of the canal below you on your right. Ahead can be seen Alverton Hall Farm, but follow the Staffordshire Way signs to the right of it and cross a large field to the field boundary on your left. Follow this round to a stile close to a large oak tree. After ascending the stile the Staffordshire Way continues to your left, but your route is to your right beside a wall on your right. Gain a stile on your right after 150 yards, and a further 100 yards

- Continued opposite -

ALTON AND BRADLEY IN THE MOORS - 8 MILES

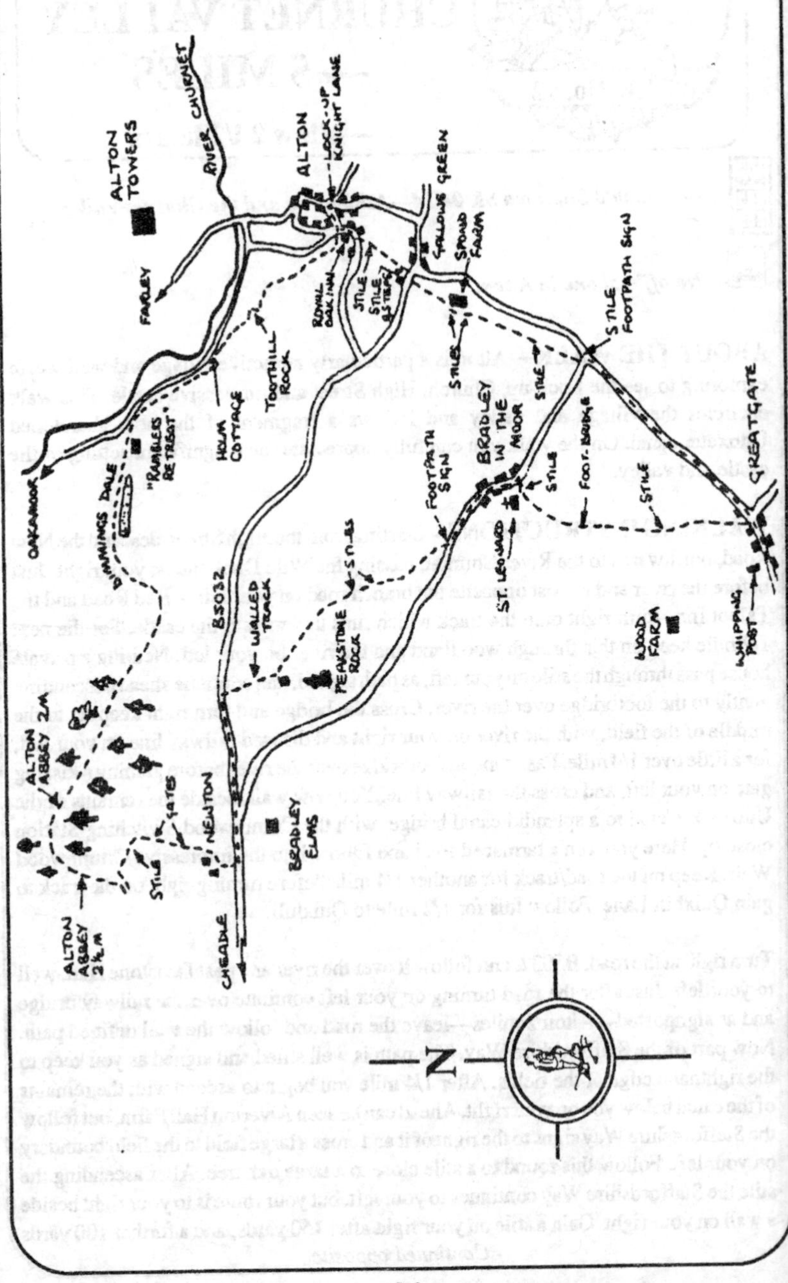

ALTON AND BRADLEY IN THE MOORS —8 MILES

—allow 4 hours

1:25,000—Sheet No 04/14—Ashbourne and the Churnet Valley.

—No official one in Alton.

ABOUT THE WALK—A longer walk than most in the book but a grandslam of the area, illustrating its diverse walking potential. First you gain Toothill Rock for the area's finest view over the River Churnet, Alton Towers and to Alton Castle. From here you descend to the incomparable Dimmings Dale before ascending to the plateau and crossing the fields to Bradley in the Moors. Here you visit an unspoilt church before crossing further fields to Great Gate to see its whipping post. A short road walk from here could extend the walk by a mile to visit Croxden Abbey. You return over the fields to Gallows Green and its legends before descending to central Alton where the walk began.

WALKING INSTRUCTIONS—Starting from the lockup in Alton descend Knight Lane beside it. At the bottom cross the road with the Royal Oak Inn on your left and follow the signposted bridleway—Toothill. This walled track soon swings to your right and reaches Toothill Wood (National Trust property) a little over 1/4 mile later. Turn right at the stile to the rocks and viewpoint. Then descend the path underneath the rocks to your left before bearing right down to the road beside path sign—Alton 1/2 mile. Turn right then left on the track beside Holm Cottage, signposted Smeltmill 1/2 mile and Dimmingsdale 3/4 mile. Continue through woodland, and where the track bears left 1/4 mile later turn right and descend the path to the Rambler's Retreat Restaurant.

Walk past the restaurant on the track, keeping to the lefthand side. First pass the ruined Smeltmill before the millpond. Just after you bear left into Dimmings Dale, keeping to the lefthand side of the dale. For the next mile you keep to the dale floor, and after passing some ponds on your right the track begins to climb out of the dale, still in woodland. You soon pass a square metal mile marker—Alton Abbey 2 miles. Shortly afterwards the track swings left and away from the dale and in 1/2 mile passes another marker, Alton Abbey 2 1/2 miles. Just after the track turns sharp right and on your left can be seen your next path. Follow this first above the track before ascending through woodland to a stile. Cross the field beyond to a farm track with pond beyond. Turn right and follow this well stiled track past the houses of Newton to the B5032 road.

Turn left and follow the Alton road keeping left at the road junction. A little over 1/4 mile later turn right onto a walled track and follow this to the entrance to the houses. Go through the gate on your left and cross the field to the bottom righthand corner, on the left of the houses. Ascend the wooden stile and turn right to the next field, where you turn left keeping the field boundary on your left. This is the only part of the walk not well stiled. Ascend another wooden stile and in the subsequent field bear right to the gate. Beyond on your right is a very clear stone stile, while well to your right can be seen the impressive Peakstone Rock. Turn right through the stile and the following stiles can be seen ahead. In the next field keep the field boundary on your left to the next stile. In the final field you descend to the road, gained by a stile beside a footpath sign. The tower of Bradley in the Moors church (St Leonards) is a useful guide on this section.

Turn left along the road and walk through the village turning right up the track on the left of the church. Immediately on your left is the stone stile and path to Great Gate. A little further up the track on your right is the church gate. Through the stile, keep in the middle of the field and descend to the stream, bearing left in the bottom to the stone slab footbridge. Ascend beyond, passing a small pond on your right before gaining a wall which you keep on your immediate right to a stile. Cross a track beside a house, and keep the hedge on your right as you descend to the crossroads in Great Gate. To visit the whipping post which is beside the road, turn right. To visit Croxden Abbey turn left.

For your return follow the Alton Road for 3/4 mile, first descending to a stream and then ascending to the Bradley road junction. On the corner is the stile and path sign for Alton. Continue ahead across the field to a stile beside a gate before ascending the field heading for a large modern farm building. Ascend the stile in the fence before finding the next stile on the immediate left of the building. Just after cross the footbridge to another stile and turn right, keeping the fence on your right to reach the stile and footpath sign at the road junction at Gallows Green. Cross the road to some stone steps leading to a stile. Keep the field boundary on your right as you descend to another stile. Beyond gain a road which you follow to your right back into Alton and the Royal Oak Inn. Turn right opposite and ascend Knight Lane back to the Lockup where you began.

ALTON—unspoilt village well worth exploring. The castle site dates back to Saxon times. The principal builder was Bertram de Verdun in the 12th century, but little remains today. The present building now a preparatory school was built in the 1840's and designed by Pugin. He was very active on the other side of the valley building Alton Towers for the Shrewsbury's. Following a visit to Germany, the Earl of Shrewsbury decided that the ruined castle should be rebuilt like a German Rhineland one, the result today is very similar. Near the centre of the village is the Round House, the village lockup built in 1830. Alton Towers is the work of the Earls of Shrewsbury. The gardens are considered to be the finest in the country and are the work of Capability Brown. Today they are part of a leisure park; Britain's answer to Disneyland,USA.

Caldon Canal - Leek Branch - view from tunnel to Leek and The Roaches.

Caldon Canal - balance bridge.

OAKAMOOR & FARLEY - 5 MILES

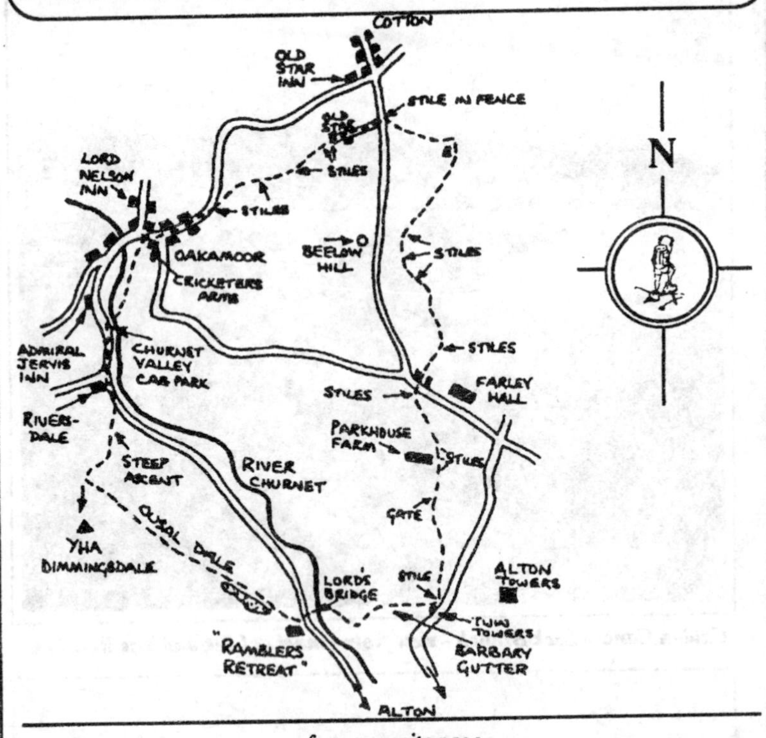

- from opposite page -

other side gain a tarred road and keep ahead to the building on your left. Here leave the road and ascend the short hill and descend the field to its bottom righthand corner, where there is a stile. The next is through the metal fence! At the road the Ye Olde Star Inn is on your right. Cross the road to walled track and follow it to Star Green Farm with the stile on the right. The next is opposite before following a walled track to another stile. You now begin descending more steeply to another stile. Continue descending, and where the field boundary turns right go through the gap and descend to your left to the road and stile. Turn left and descend Star Bank to Oakamoor. Just before the bridge over the Churnet River turn left and cross the picnic area back to the car park.

OAKAMOOR—opposite the car park, the grassy picnic area is the site of Thomas Bolton's copper works. Oakamoor had been a major industrial area for several centuries. In 1790 Thomas Patten and Co had a large copper-rolling mill. Later this was purchased by Bolton's who in 1856 produced the first Atlantic cable here. The firm expanded considerably but a century later in 1963 it was closed down and business was concentrated at the huge Froghall works.

FARLEY HALL—formerly owned by the Shrewsbury family but now a private residence. During World War 11 it served as a Youth Hostel.

OAKAMOOR AND FARLEY — 5 MILES

—allow 2 1/2 hours

—1:25,000 Sheet No SK 04/14—Ashbourne and The Churnet Valley.

—Oakamoor—Churnet Valley car park & picnic site. Near Rambler's Retreat restaurant.

ABOUT THE WALK—You begin with a steep ascent through woodland to gain Ousal Dale and the descent to Lord's Bridge. Here another, but gentler ascent brings you to Farley and its hall. Pleasant level walking across fields and woodland takes you to Old Star and the descent to Oakamoor. The walk can be extended by 1/2 mile to include Dimmings Dale via the YHA and to visit the 16th century Ye Olde Star Inn at Cotton.

WALKING INSTRUCTIONS—From the Churnet Valley car park turn left along the road for 1/4 mile to the road junction beside Rivesdale House. Bear left and 100 yards later, with retention walling just ahead, turn right and begin ascending steeply through the woodland of Moss Banks. At the top close to a cottage bear right to a stile and walled track. Follow this to your right to the junction of the Staffordshire Way and YHA turn off. Turn left to descend Ousal Dale, taking the middle track in a few yards. If walking the slightly longer route continue ahead past the YHA and descend into Dimmings Dale. Turn left and follow the path to the Smeltingmill and Rambler's Retreat restaurant. Both routes join here.

Cross the road and Lords Bridge over the Churnet River. Over the railway line (disused) the path bears right before turning left and ascending through woodland past a chained oak on your left. At the top you reach a twin-towered house. The stile is on the lefthandside; on your right is Farley Lane and Alton Towers. You are now heading due north first to a stile then into Farley Park, ascending between fir trees to the righthand side of Parkhouse Farm. The path is not defined but all the stiles are there. Past the farm you can see Farley Hall ahead and bear half left across the field, ascending to its top lefthand corner. Her are two stiles before gaining the road at Farley. Go straight across and up the road past Cliffe Cottage. At the top ascend a stile followed by another and bear left keeping to the edge of woodland.

Leaving the woodland after a stile, continue ahead to another before bearing right and ascending over the ridge to the gate on the righthand side of a derelict cottage. The

- continued opposite -

OAKAMOOR & WHISTON - 8 MILES

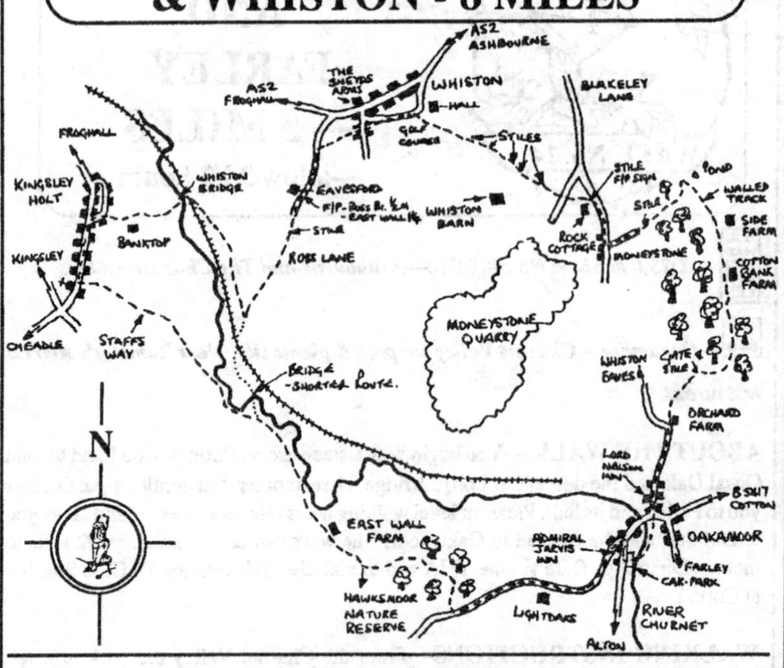

- from opposite page -

centre of Whiston with the Sneyds Arms, turn left down the path opposite the house named Sans Sougi. After a few yards cross the road and walk down Brooklands Close. At the end on the right of High Winds is the path which soon swings left to a stile and another stile onto the walled track of Ross Lane.Turn left along the lane and at Eavesford pass the sign—Ross Bridge 1/2 mile and East Wall 11/4 miles. The latter would be that distance if the bridge over the Churnet was there; instead you will have to do a 11/4 miles extra to get there. Keep on the lane for 1/2 mile to woodland close to Ross Bridge. Here turn right onto a track through the woodland, heading northwards close to the railway line on your left. After 1/2 mile pass under it and over Whiston Bridge over the River Churnet. Continue and ascend past Banktop to the housing estate of Kingsley Holt.

At the main road turn left through the village for about 1/4 mile to the church on your right. Here as Staffordshire Way signed turn left and begin descending the fields towards the River Churnet more than 1/2 mile away. The river keeps you company for almost 1/2 mile before you head towards East Wall Farm. It is on this stretch that the pathline from Ross Bridge joins your route.Keep to the righthand side of the farm, with its pond on your right. Continue ahead on a track into Hawksmoor Nature Reserve and wood. Just inside the trees where the tracks fork, take the left one and follow it for 1/2 mile to the B5417 road. Turn left and descend the road back into Oakamoor, just over 1/2 mile away with the car park on your right, just past Admiral Jarvis Inn.

OAKAMOOR AND WHISTON —8 MILES

—allow 3 1/2 hours

—1:25,000 Sheet No SK 04/14—Ashbourne and the Churnet Valley.

—Oakamoor—Churnet Valley car park & picnic site.

ABOUT THE WALK—a mixture of woodland and high level walking with walled lanes and the Churnet Valley. The walk is slightly longer than most, largely due to the nonexistent footbridge over the River Churnet near Ross Bridge, at the time of writing in 1986. However there is now a bridge and you can reduce the walk by two miles; but I still prefer the longer route! It is a delightful walk with an inn almost halfway!

WALKING INSTRUCTIONS—From the car park cross the bridge over the river and bear left across the field/picnic area to the righthand side of Oakamoor bridge. Cross the B5417 road and continue ahead past the Lord Nelson inn. Continue up the narrow road for a little over 1/4 mile to the sharp lefthand bend and Orchard Farm. Leave the road and keep ahead between the houses on the track, bearing right after a few yards onto a walled track, which you follow to woodland. Here turn right on a track in the trees, and after 60 yards near the crest of the valley don't descend but bear left on the track which you follow almost due north for the next mile. After 1/4 mile you emerge from the trees and walk beside the woodland on your immediate left. Pass Cotton Bank Farm then Side Farm on your right. 1/4 mile later, with a pond on your right leave the track on your left via a stile and ascend a faint path through the trees. At the top it becomes more defined as you continue through more pine trees to a stile on the forest edge. Here you keep a wall on your right as you head towards a track at Moneystone. Upon reaching the minor road, opposite a telephone kiosk, turn right.

Keep on this road for 1/4 mile to the stile and footpath sign on your left just past the aptly named Rock Cottage. Turn left and cross the field slightly to your right to another stile. Beyond is another and abandoned road. On your left is a quarry. Keep ahead into Black Plantation, on a path keeping the wall on your immediate right. The path is well stiled and on your left can be seen Whiston Barn. After the fifth stile you cross a golf course, passing a gritstone boulder on your left. Gain the minor road with the Club House—Whiston Hall—on your right. Turn left along the road and just before the

- continued opposite -

DIMMINGS DALE & OUSAL DALE - 2 & 3 1/2 MILES

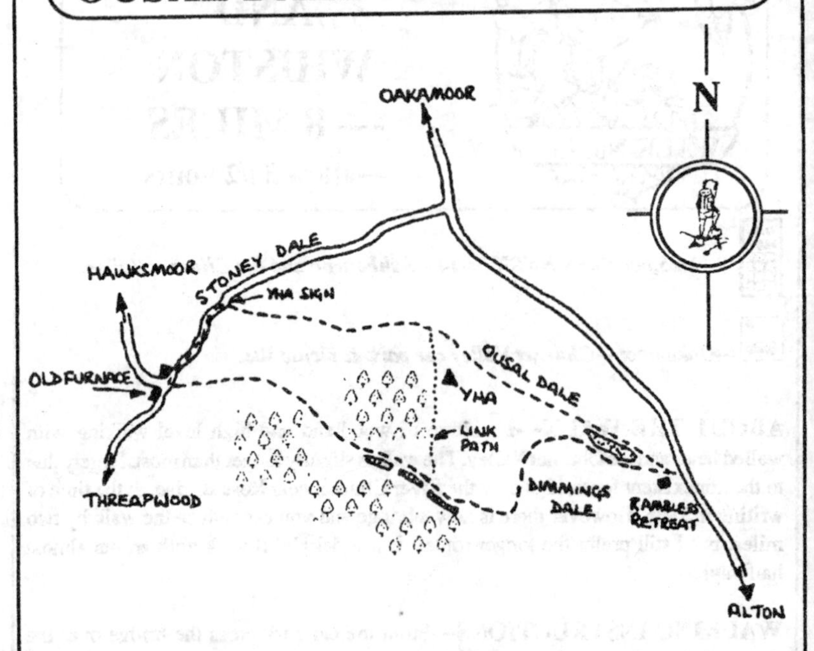

Castern Hall, nr. Ilam.

DIMMINGS DALE AND OUSAL DALE —2 & 3 1/2 MILES

—allow 1/2 hours

— 1:25,000 Pathfinder Sheet No SK 04/14—Ashbourne and the Churnet Valley.

—no official one but parking room at start of walk near Rambler's Retreat restaurant.

ABOUT THE WALK—Dimmings Dale provides some of the finest walking in the area in delectable woodlands, with ponds and rhododendrons. This walk takes you first up the dale to Oldfurnace where a short road walk brings you to the track with extensive views before descending Ousal Dale back to your start. The route to Oldfurnace and back is 3 1/2 miles long. The 2 mile walk uses the path past Dimmingsdale YHA (The Ranger) as the cross link to Ousal Dale.

WALKING INSTRUCTIONS—From the Rambler's Retreat restaurant keep on the lefthand track, soon passing the remains of the Smelting mill on your right, before the millpond. Shortly after the track turns left into Dimmings Dale and a path can be seen on either side of the dale. Follow the righthand one, and in 1/2 mile just after the first pond on your left is the path to the YHA and Ousal Dale. Here the shorter route ascends while the longer continues in the dale passing more ponds on your left. Little over 1/2 mile later reach the road junction at Oldfurnace.

Turn right onto the Oakamoor road and 1/4 mile later take the track on your right. First heading across the fields on the walled track for 1/2 mile, following the Staffordshire Way, to the signpost and junction with the YHA turn off. Here the shorter route joins the main route. Continue ahead on the Staffordshire Way descending immediately into Ousal Dale. Keep to the middle track past and through woodland, with views to Alton Castle ahead. 1/2 mile later reach the Smelting mill pond and just after the Rambler's Retreat restaurant.

DIMMINGSDALE - millponds and former corn mill can still be seen. In the 18th. century a lead smelting mill was active here.

HAWKSMOOR - 4 MILES

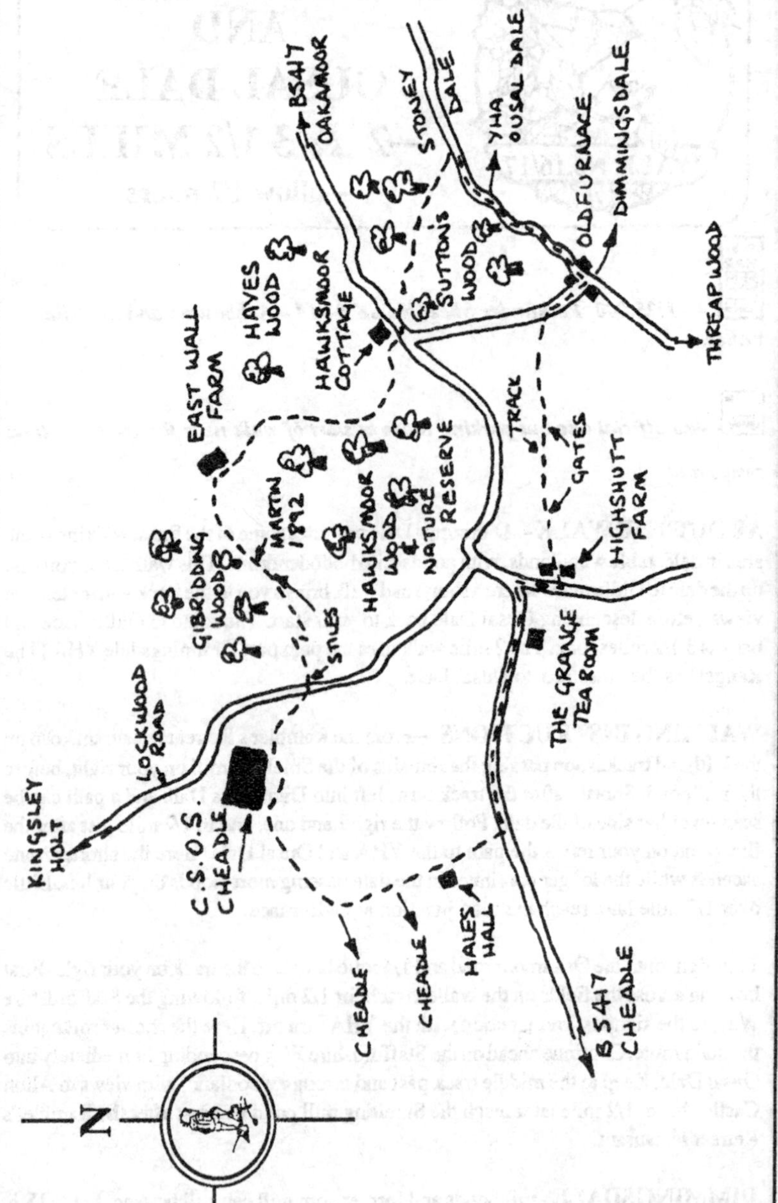

HAWKSMOOR NATURE RESERVE—250 acres and officially opened in 1933. More than 40 species of birds have been sighted here.

HAWKSMOOR —4 MILES

—Allow 2 hours

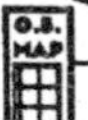—*1:25,000—Sheet No 04/14—Ashbourne and the Churnet Valley.*

—*No official one; nearest at Oakamoor.*

ABOUT THE WALK—a very enjoyable walk with a mixture of beautiful woodland, high open views, historical buildings and dales. The walk can be walked in its own right or as an extension to the Dimmings Dale or Oakamoor walks. For convenience I have started the walk details from Hawksmoor but being circular you can join it at Oldfurnace or by walking the B5417 or Stoney Dale lane from Oakamoor; this will add on an extra couple of miles.

WALKING INSTRUCTIONS—At the crest of the B5417 road, opposite Greendale Lane, turn right through the stone pillared entrance into Hawksmoor Wood and Nature Reserve. The track is well defined as you immediately descend to your left through the trees. At the bottom and a little over 1/2 mile gain East Wall Farm, and guided by the signs walk around its lefthand side. Keep left of the pond following a path which gradually ascends with Gibridding Wood on your immediate right. After 1/4 mile pass the solitary gravestone to Martin, 1892 . Just after pass through a stile and follow a grass track still ascending gently to Lockwood Road, 1/4 mile away; reached via a stile.

Cross the road and walk along the drive towards the masts and radio station of C.S.O.S. Cheadle, a miniature Cheltenham GCHQ. You keep on this drive following it round to your left past the buildings and pond. After 1/2 mile at the junction with the Woodheadhall Farm drive on your right, keep ahead on the tarmaced road to pass Hales Hall on your right—now a caravan and camp site— and reach the B5417 Cheadle Road. Turn left along the road passing the entrance to Lower Grange Farm on your right before the Grange Tea Room on your right. Shortly afterwards at the road junction with the impressive rock outcrop of Highshutt on your left, turn right on the Alton road—3 3/4 miles—and 30 yards later turn left at Highshutt Farm and walk through the farmyard and descend the fields, mostly on a track, keeping the field boundary on your right. A little over 1/2 mile gain Greendale Lane and turn right for Oldfurnace, 100 yards away. Turn left and follow the Stoney Dale lane which ascends towards woodland. After 1/4 mile pass the track and path sign to Oakamoor Youth Hostel, and 100 yards later on your left is the ascending track through Sutton's Wood, which will lead you back to Hawksmoor, 1/2 mile away. Back at the start you pass the footpath sign—Stoney Dale 1/2 mile.

ECTON AND THE MANIFOLD VALLEY - 2 WALKS - 4 MILES

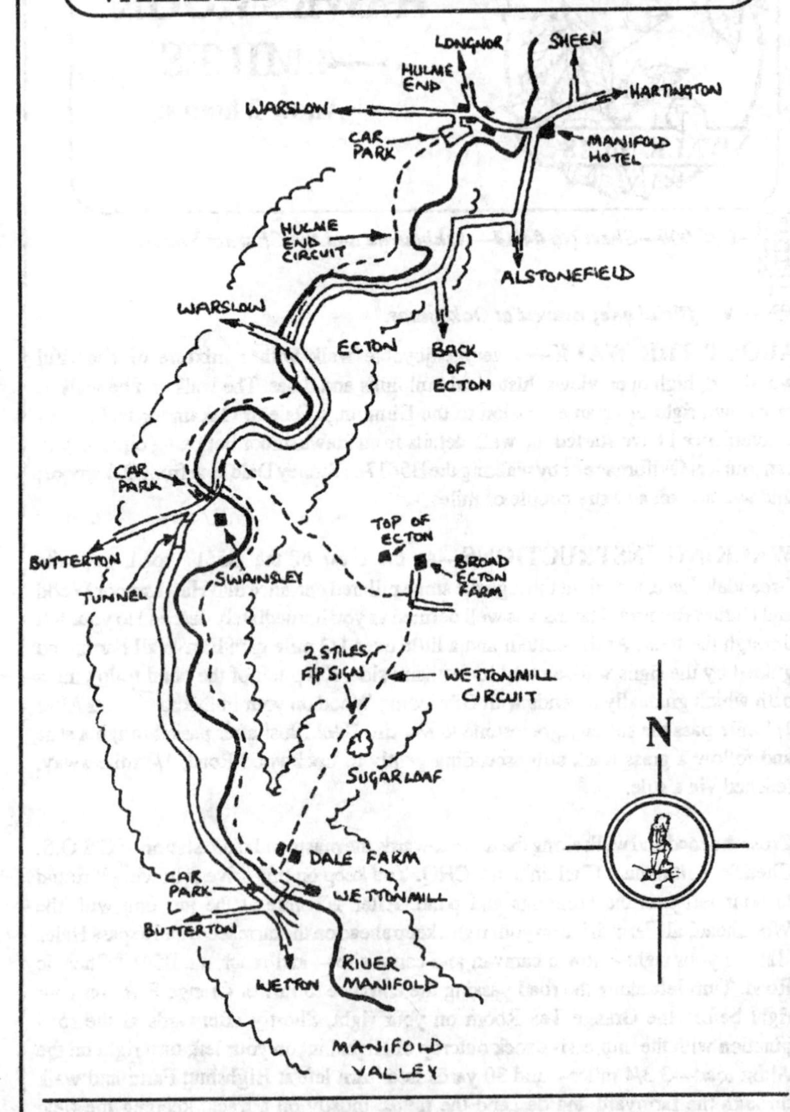

MANIFOLD VALLEY LIGHT RAILWAY—running between Waterhouses and Hulme was a remarkable railway, opened in June 1904, at a cost of £4,000 per mile. The trains travelled at a maximum speed of 25 m.p.h. and were Indian in style. The line was intended to carry dairy products and limestone but was never a commercial success and closed in 1934. The Staffordshire County Council purchased it and converted the line to pedestrian use.

ECTON AND THE MANIFOLD VALLEY —TWO WALKS —4 MILES EACH

— allow 2 hours each

—1:25,000 Outdoor Leisure Map—The While Peak—(West Sheet).

—beside Manifold trail near Ecton Bridge.—Wettonmill.—Hulme End.

ABOUT THE WALKS—The first details a walk above the valley to Top of Ecton and down a dale to Wettonmill. From here you return along the valley floor on the original Wettonmill road. There is a tea room at Wettonmill. The second walk is along the Manifold Trail to its end at Hulme End where the valley opens out. You return the same way. Both walks explore the beauty of the Manifold Valley.

WALKING INSTRUCTIONS—Wettonmill circuit.
From the car park near Ecton Bridge return to the road and turn left over the bridge. 200 yards later turn right over the stile and begin ascending to your right up the grass pathway. After 1/4 mile keep the wall on your immediate right and soon begin to descend. In the third field bear right to cross two fields with Summerhill Farm well to your right. Join the farm track from the farm and descend to the farm road junction. Turn right along the drive and where it turns left continue ahead, keeping the wall on your right as you continue descending. At the end of the third field keep the fence on your left to reach a couple of stiles a little further on. Continue ahead passing the limestone mound of Sugarloaf on your left and descend to Dale Farm, just over 1/4 mile away. Pass through the farm to the road. To your left is Wettonmill. Turn right and keep on the unfenced track above the river for the next I 1/2 miles to the road near Ecton Bridge. Turn left then right back to the car park.

WALKING INSTRUCTIONS—Hulme End Circuit.
Walk out the top end of the car park onto the tarmaced path and follow it for the next two miles to its end at the car park close to Hulme End. Return the same way.

WETTONMILL—a former cornmill. Close by the river Manifold disappears down a swallet and reappears at the bubble holes near Ilam Hall, five miles away.

ECTON—the copper mines here were particularly rich and at their peak yielded 12 tons a year. They were finally closed in 1890.

WETTON & THOR'S CAVE - 4 1/2 MILES

THOR'S CAVE—the opening facing the valley is 23 feet wide by 30 feet high. Excavations have revealed that it has been occupied from the Bronze Age to Saxon times. Many of the artifacts can be seen in Derby Museum. Close to the start of the ascent by the river is a further cave, known as Donkey Hole or Radcliffe Cave. Here a person named Radcliffe hid his horse when Bonnie Prince Charles was marching through the area in 1745.

WETTON AND THOR'S CAVE —4 1/2 MILES

—allow 2 hours

—*1:25,000 Outdoor Leisure Map—The White Peak (West Sheet).*

—*Wetton and Wettonmill.*

ABOUT THE WALK—The walk can be started from either Wetton or Wettonmill, but for the purposes of writing and the way I walk the route, I have started the description from Wetton. The walk is full of superlatives with the majestic natural feature of Thor's Cave dominating the whole route. The view from here of the Manifold Valley is second to none. At Wettonmill there is a tearoom to fortify you for the walk over the tops back to Wetton!

WALKING INSTRUCTIONS—Turn right out of the car park and at the crossroads take the walled lane on your left signposted—'Thor's Cave, Concession Path—at own risk.' Keep on the track for just over 1/4 mile to a stile. Over this turn right at the next stile and follow the defined path round to Thor's Cave. Here you join the major path from the Manifold Valley. Descend this path and steps to the valley floor and turn right. 1/2 mile later reach the minor road; cross it and keep on the righthand one to reach Wettonmill 1/2 mile later, via the bridge.

Over the bridge turn left and follow the track to Dale Farm. Here leave the track and walk through the farm, path signed—Back of Ecton 1 1/4 miles. The path ascends a shallow dale heading for the limestone outcrop, Sugarloaf. Keep to the lefthand side of this to reach two stiles and a footpath sign. Bear right and keep the fence on your right to the next stile. Here the field boundary—a wall—is now on your left as you ascend gently to the track near Top of Ecton. Turn right along the track and follow it over the hill and at the junction beyond, turn right and leave the track and descend to two stiles. Over these bear right across the open field heading for the saddle on the left of Wetton Hill. The pathline is faint but the wall in the saddle acts as a guide, 1/2 mile away. Keep the wall on your right to a stile. In the next field the stile, a wooden one, is partway along on your left. Over this you ascend to your right slightly before descending to a stile and reservoir beyond. Here you join a track and descend into Wetton. Continue ahead past the Royal Oak inn on your right and a little further turn right back to the car park.

HAMPS VALLEY & MUSDEN WOOD - 6 or 8 MILES

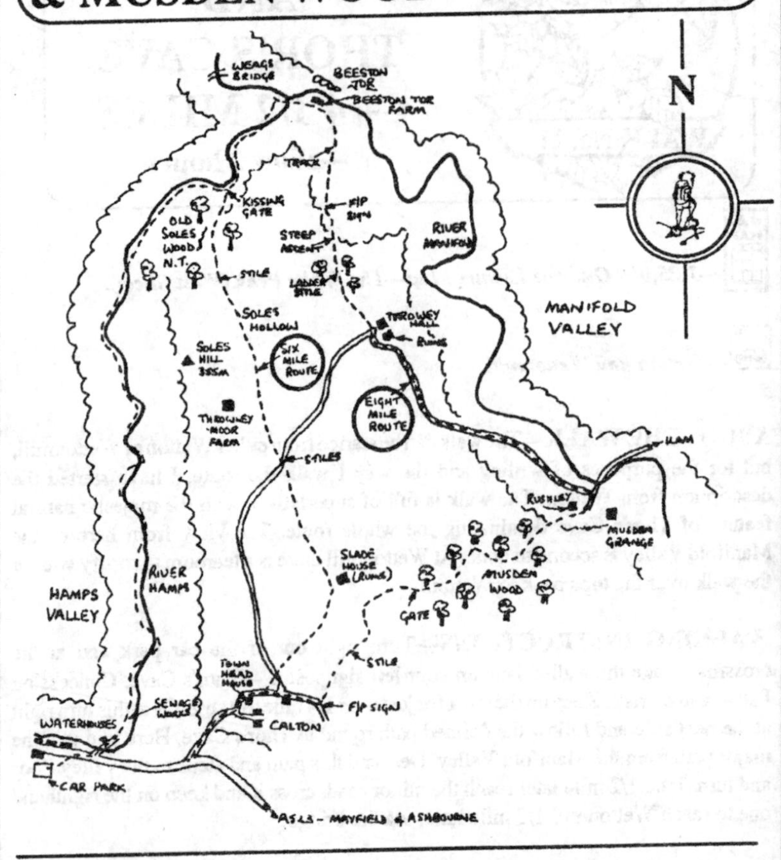

WALKING INSTRUCTIONS—8 mile route.

Follow the 6 mile walk instructions to Old Sole Wood turn off. Here you continue on the tarmaced track for another 1/2 mile before turning right through a gate to reach the track close to Beeston Tor Farm; opposite is the Tor. Follow the track to your right as it ascends over the fields for 1/2 mile to a footpath sign. Here you ascend steeply to the trees and a ladder stile. Over this descend ahead before bearing left towards Throwley Hall, reached via stile. Turn right then left onto the minor road and follow it for a little over a mile to the junction at Rushley. Turn right and reach the signposted path—Calton 1 1/2 miles. The path enters Musden Wood, and for the next 1 1/2 mile you are in woodland, keeping to the valley floor. You emerge from the trees at a stile and keep the field boundary on your left for just 1/4 mile to the minor road in Calton and path sign. Turn right and follow the road round to your left, ignoring the turning to your right. At the end of the road reach Town Head House, joining the route of the 6 mile walk. Follow the road round to your left then right and descend to the A523 road and Waterhouses.

HAMPS VALLEY AND MUSDEN WOOD —6 OR 8 MILES

—allow 3 to 4 hours

- 1:25,000 Outdoor Leisure Map—The White Peak (West Sheet)

—Waterhouses

ABOUT THE WALK—The Hamps Valley is a particularly attractive valley with steep sides and woodland. Meandering spasmodically is the River Hamps, which like the Manifold often runs underground during the summer. After walking much of the Hamps Valley you have a choice of return routes; both have their attractions. The 6 mile route is through Old Soles Wood and Soles Hollow and is a peaceful and remote walk to Calton where the longer route comes in. This 8 mile route allows you to see the impressive limestone face of Beeston Tor before ascending to Throwley Hall. A road walk down the Manifold Valley to Rushley is followed by a walk through Musden Wood to Calton.

WALKING INSTRUCTIONS—6 mile route

Walk through the car park past the Silver Jubilee Memorial onto the line of the railway following a path for a short distance before descending to the A523 road. Turn right and shortly afterwards left into the Hamps Valley (Manifold Track). You keep on the tarmaced surface for the next 2 1/2 miles. First passing a cycle hire store on your left and the sewage works on your right! After 2 1/2 miles you reach on your right a kissing gate and National Trust sign—Old Soles Wood. Leave the tarmaced path here and go through the kissing gate and follow the defined ascending path up a shallow valley in the woodland. After 1/2 mile emerge from the trees at a stile and continue ascending in Soles Hollow with the-wall on your left. 1/4 mile later after a gate the wall is now on your right, and ahead on your right can be seen Throwleymoor Farm. Continue ahead passing three dew ponds before reaching the minor road. Cross to the stile and keep the wall on your left to another pond 1/4 mile away. Here the pathline becomes a track with the wall on your right as you descend to Slade House. Bear right through the gate on the track, and at the next stile right again with a pond on your left. The track soon becomes walled as you approach Caldon. Upon reaching the minor road, cross to the stile and cross two fields to another stile and turn right into central Caldon. Here the Musden Wood route joins. Continue along the road to Town Head House and follow the road round to your left before turning right and descending to the A523 road. Turn right and soon pass the entrance to Hamps Valley on your right and a little later the path on your left back to the car park.

WATERHOUSES AND CAULDON - 2 MILES

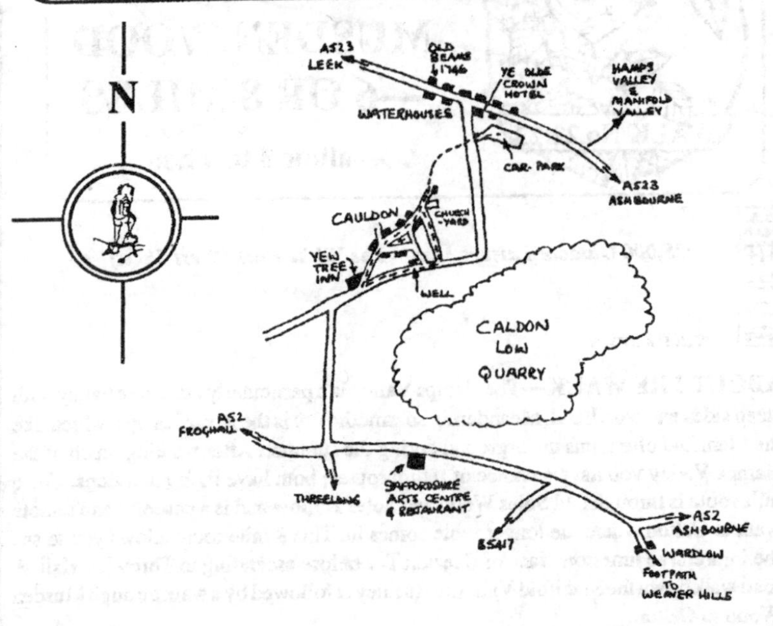

Cauldon quarry.

WATERHOUSES AND CAULDON — 2 MILES

—allow 1 hour

O.S. MAP

1:25,000—Outdoor Leisure map—The White Peak (West Sheet)
1:25,000—Pathfinder Series—Sheet No 04/14— Ashbourne and the Churnet Valley.

—Waterhouses.

ABOUT THE WALK—a very short walk—to the pub and back! The aim principally is to see Cauldon—a particularly attractive village, lying very close to, but hidden from, a massive limestone quarry.

WALKING INSTRUCTIONS—Walk down the entrance drive of the car-park to the minor road. Opposite on your right, near the railway bridge is the tarmaced path to Cauldon. Follow this and after 1/2 mile gain the walled lane on the outskirts of Cauldon. Follow this past the churchyard on your left and bear right to the church. Past it bear right again through the village to minor road and Yew Tree Inn. Walk down the road to a well on your left - *'Thy Clouds Drop Fatness, 1878'*. Just afterwards turn left and regain the churchyard and your earlier path. Retrace your steps back to Waterhouses car park. Waterhouses too is worth exploring for the Old Beams dated 1746 and an inn called Ye Olde Crown Hotel. The car park is also the bike hiring station for exploring the Manifold Valley—called a track - just like New Zealand! Another cycle hire store is at the start of the valley.

Thor's Cave - see Wetton walk.

HARTINGTON, BERESFORD DALE & BIGGIN DALE - 5 MILES

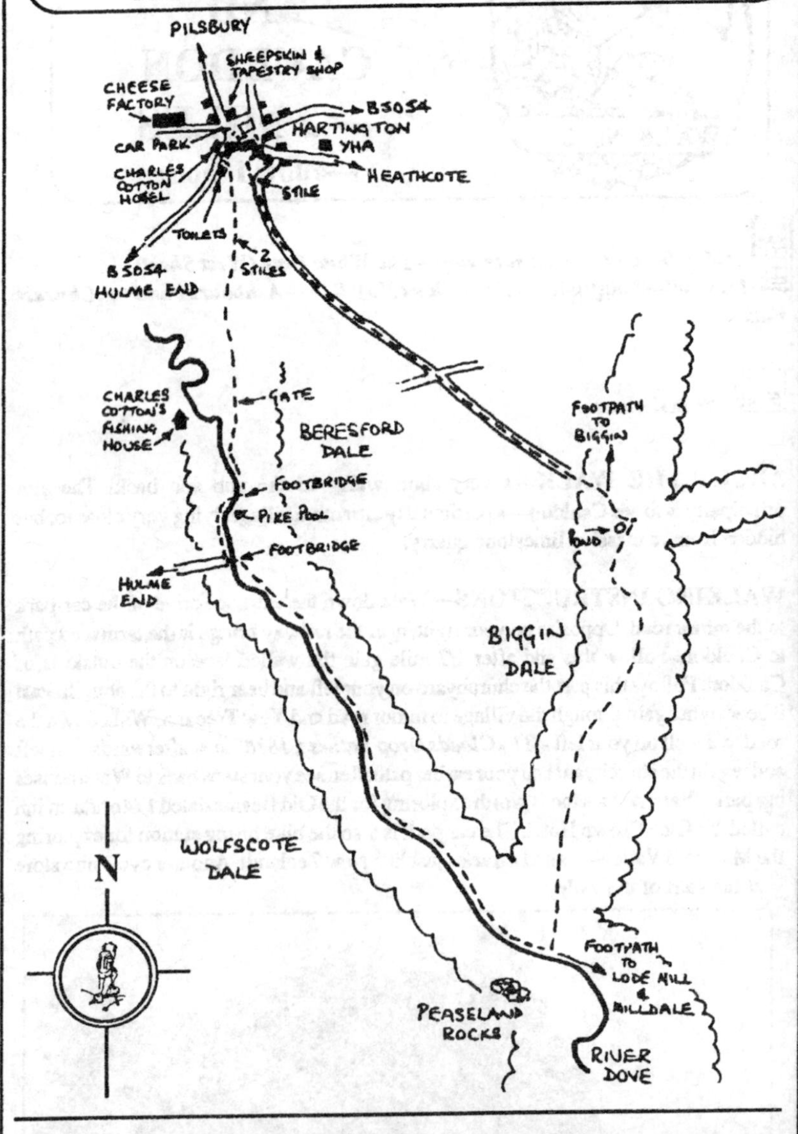

CHARLES COTTON—the River Dove is synonymous with the fishing skills of Charles Cotton and Izaak Walton, who wrote the Compleat Angler in 1653. A fishing temple where they met still remains, on private property. Here Charles Cotton would rest and smoke his pipe, referring to it as 'his breakfast.' Little remains of Beresford Hall where Cotton was born in 1630.

HARTINGTON, BERESFORD DALE & BIGGIN DALE— 5 MILES

—allow 2 1/2 hours

—O.S. 1:25,000 Outdoor Leisure Map—The White Peak—(West Sheet).

—Market Place and Parson's Field, Hartington.

ABOUT THE WALK—an exceptional walk through three limestone dales.In Beresford Dale and Wolfscote Dale you walk beside the River Dove. In Biggin Dale, a dry dale, you ascend to the limestone plateau and cross the lanes back to Hartington. The village is well worth exploring at the end to see the church, eat a cream tea or purchase some famous Stilton cheese.

WALKING INSTRUCTIONS—Turn right out of the Market Place past the Charles Cotton Hotel on your right to the Public Toilets on your left shortly afterwards. Here as signed turn left onto the path for Beresford Dale. Past the toilets you bear right to two stiles across a track before entering large open fields and the defined path, making its way across them into woodland. In the woodland the river Dove joins you on your right. Cross the footbridge and keep the river on your left to the next footbridge 1/4 mile later. Cross this and bear right across the field to a stile and the well used path by the river. On your left is a limestone outcrop with caves. Keep beside the river for the next 1 1/2 mile as you walk through Wolfscote Dale.

After I 1/2 miles, at the entrance to Biggin Dale on your left, turn left and begin the gentle ascent of the dale, keeping to its base for 11/4 miles. Where the dale forks keep left and as footpath signed ascend out of the dale to a stile. Here you gain a walled track which you follow for over 1/2 mile to a minor road and cross roads. Keep ahead on the tarmaced road for 3/4 mile, and close to Hartington at a sharp righthand bend leave the road at the stile and descend into Hartington. Bear right then left at the bottom to reach the edge of the Market Place and car park.

HARTINGTON—the only place in Derbyshire making cheeses. In the 19th century Derbyshire at South Longford had the first cheese factory in England. The church dedicated to St. Giles dates from the 13th century. Inside is the only complete set of panels representing the patriarchs of Israel and a memorial to Thomas Mellor who died aged 103.

ALSTONEFIELD & MILLDALE - 4 MILES

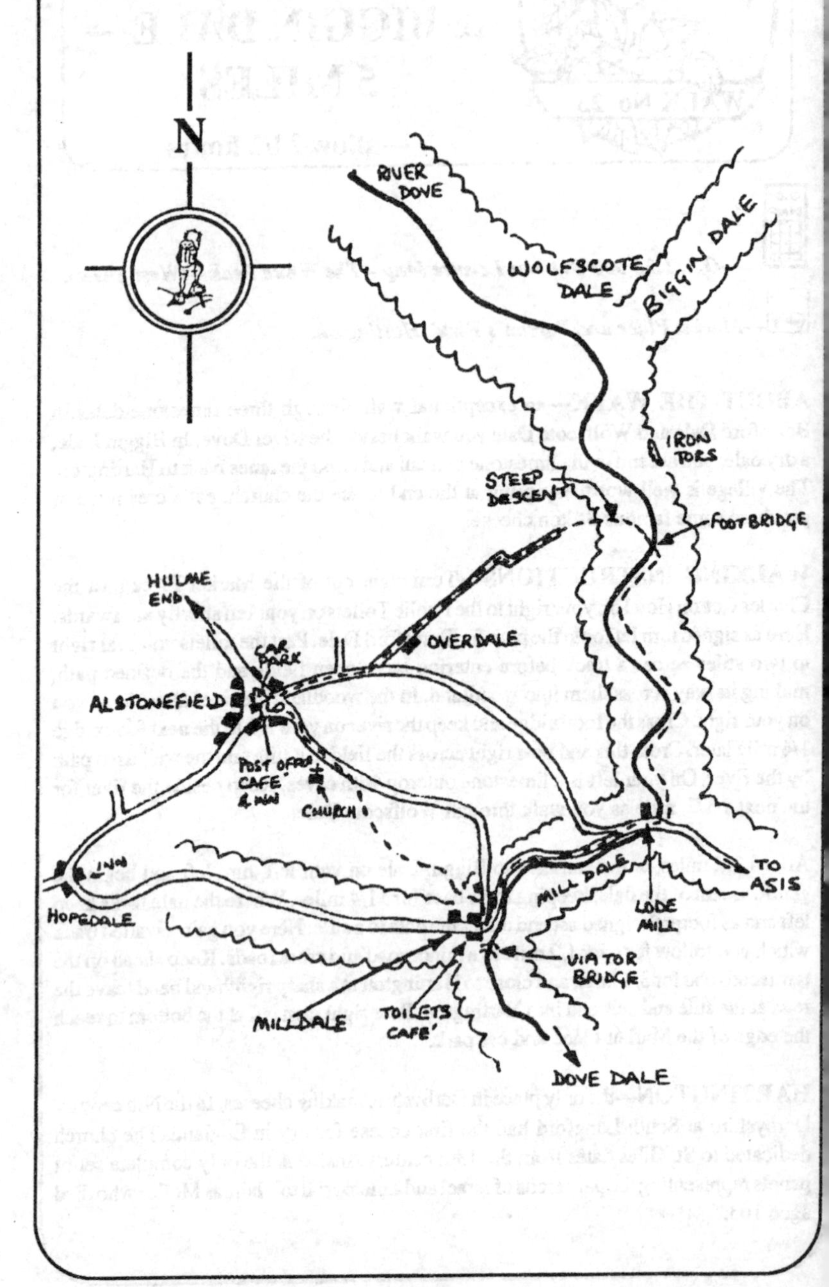

ALSTONEFIELD AND MILLDALE - 4 MILES

- allow 2 hours

- 1.25,000 Outdoor Leisure Map The White Peak - West Sheet.

—Alstonefield

ABOUT THE WALK—Alstonefield is one of the prettiest villages in Staffordshire and is best left to explore at the end of the walk. First you cross the fields to a magnificent view point over Wolfscote Dale and the river Dove. You descend and walk beside it to Lode Mill and Milldale where there is a tea room. A short ascent returns you to Alstonefield and its church.

WALKING INSTRUCTIONS—Turn right out of the car park and left shortly afterwards on the Lode Mill/Milldale road. Keep on this out of the village for just over 1/4 mile and take the second walled track on your left. First you pass Overdale and in just over 112 mile later gain the edge of Wolfscote Dale. The descent is steep, curving to your right down to the footbridge. Cross the river and turn right to join the well used path beside the river on your right Keep on this path for 3/4 mile to the road and bridge at Lode Mill. Turn right over the bridge and left long the road to Milldale. In the hamlet turn right and right again, and after a few yards, instead of ascending the road, take the path on your left and ascend the fields, bearing right at the top to the road. Turn left to pass the church and gain the greens and inn of Alstonefield. Keep ahead to the main road with the car park just ahead.

ALSTONEFIELD - winner of the best kept village award, with well kept greens and attractive houses. The church dates from Norman times but is largely 15th century. Inside are carved 17th century pews and one canopied one used by the Cotton family from Beresford Hall. Charles Cotton used this pew.

ILAM AND DOVEDALE - 7 MILES

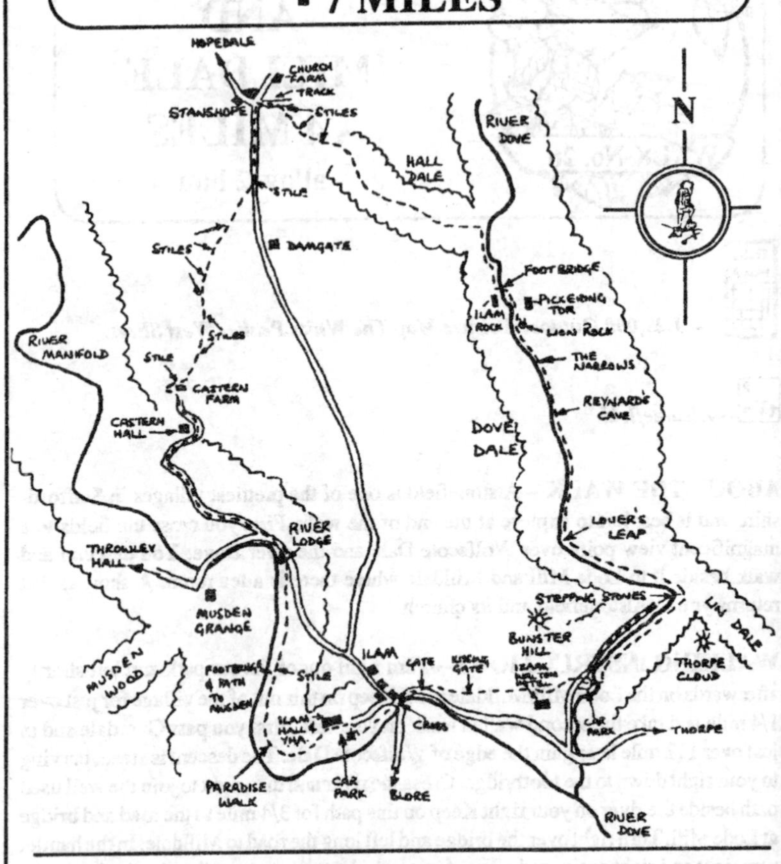

- from opposite page -

Cloud and cross them. Continue along the road to the car park on your left. Here on your right is the stile and path to Ilam. Turn right across the fields passing close to the Izaak Walton Hotel on your left before gaining a kissing gate. Beyond you keep on the defined path across another field before descending to a gate and Ilam road on your left. Turn right into Ilam and right at the Cross. Near the entrance to Ilam Hall turn left and follow the path around the house on your right to Ilam Church. A short walk from here returns you to Ilam Hall.

ILAM—Church contains a Saxon font, a tomb to St Bertram, funeral garlands and a Chantry Chapel with the reclining figure of David Pike Watts by Sir Francis Chantry. The Watts Russell family were responsible for the Ilam Hall, mostly built last century. In 1934 it was given to the National Trust who have an Information Centre here. Part of the building is now a Youth Hostel. The cross in the centre of the village was erected in 1840 in memory of Mrs. Watts Russell.

ILAM AND DOVEDALE — 7 MILES

—allow 3 hours

—1:25,000 Outdoor Leisure Map—The White Peak—(West Sheet).

—Dovedale and Ilam.

ABOUT THE WALK—The grandslam of the area. Apart from seeing the matchless beauty of Dovedale and its limestone rock formations, you explore Ilam and the River Manifold, pass the impressive Castern Hall and descend the attractive Hall Dale. Combined, one of the finest walks in the Midlands! The walk can be started at the Dovedale car park, but I prefer Ilam for its relatively quiet locality, and the walking instructions commence from there.

WALKING INSTRUCTIONS—From Ilam walk past the Hall—Youth Hostel and National Trust Information Centre—and descend the steps and curve right to the river. Walk round to your right on 'Paradise Walk', a wide path on the edge of the woodland which after 1/4 mile brings you beside the river and bubble holes. Continue to footbridge over the river. Don't cross but keep ahead through the stile and follow the private path to River Lodge. A small charge is made for walking this section. At the road turn left and right shortly afterwards to follow the ascending curving road to Castern Hall, 1/2 mile away. Keep on the road around the hall to the back of it, where turn right up the drive towards Castern Farm. Just past the first house on your right turn left and ascend the field to a stile. Turn right through this and keep the wall on your right as you head round the farm, following the path signs—Damgate. At the stile at the farm bear left to another stile just past some water springs. Over this stile keep the wall on your left and you will come to six stiles as you cross the fields well to the left of Damgate. In the seventh and largest field you gain a stile beside the minor road and turn left along it to Stanshope, 1/4 mile away.

Before the houses turn right onto a walled track, footpath signed—Milldale— and a few yards later right at the stile and path sign—Dovedale. The path is defined as you descend to the next stile and enter Hall Dale. Continue descending for 1/2 mile to the river Dove and Dovedale. Bear right at the bottom keeping the river on your left to Ilam Rock. Here cross the footbridge and turn right to continue down Dovedale with the river on your right, past Lions Rock, the Narrows, Reynards Cave and natural arch and eventually Lover's Leap. 1/2 mile later reach the stepping stones beneath Thorpe

- continued opposite -

THORPE - 3 MILES

N
DOVE DALE
BUNSTER HILL
STEPPING STONE
LIN DALE
CAR-PARK
THORPE CLOUD
IZAAK WALTON HOTEL
QUARRY
ILAM
CAR-PARK & TOILETS
TO ASIS & TISSINGTON
RIVER MANIFOLD
STILES
THORPE MILL FARM
THORPE
INN
COLDWALL BRIDGE
ST. LEONARDS
TO ASIS & ASHBOURNE
RIVER DOVE

THORPE —3 MILES

—allow 1 1/2 hours

- 1:25,000 Outdoor Leisure Map—The White Peak—(West Sheet).

—Dovedale and Thorpe.

ABOUT THE WALK—a short walk, to allow you to obtain views of Dovedale, and to explore the attractive village of Thorpe before descending an old coach road to a little used bridge over the Dove. A short walk across the fields returns you to the car park at Dovedale.

WALKING INSTRUCTIONS—From the car park you can either cross the footbridge and turn left and walk beside the river to the stepping stones and Dovedale's entrance, or return to the road and turn right and walk along it and cross the stepping stones. At the other side turn right through the kissing gate and follow the ascending path up Lin Dale. Don't get confused with the ascending path to the summit of Thorpe Cloud! The path keeps to the base of the dale for 1/2 mile before bearing right to pass a small quarry on your left before descending to your right to a stile, car park and toilets at Thorpe.

Cross the road and follow the narrow road past the houses to St. Leonard's church on your left. Continue along the road to the end of the houses and gate. Here turn right and descend the track down to Coldwall Bridge, 1/2 mile away. Don't cross the bridge but turn right onto the faint path close to the river and follow it for 1/2 mile to the Thorpe/ Ilam road, reached by a stile near Thorpe Mill Farm on your right. Opposite and a little to your left is the stile and path which is well stiled along the lefthand side of the fields. In the fourth field turn left back into the car park.

THORPE—the church dedicated to St. Leonard dates from Norman times; the tower being built about 1100. Inside is a Norman tub font, one of only three in Derbyshire. Of particular note is the tomb to John Millward erected in 1632.

COLDWALL BRIDGE—built in 1762 and part of the Blythe Marsh turnpike to Cheadle and Oakamoor in Staffordshire. A milepost can be seen—Cheadle 11 miles.

WALK RECORD CHART

Date walked -

ASHBOURNE AREA—

ASHBOURNE AND THE TISSINGTON TRAIL—6 MILES..................

MAYFIELD—5 MILES..................

OSMASTON—4 1/2 MILES..................

CALWICH ABBEY & RIVER DOVE—4 1/2 MILES..................

THECHURNETVALLEY—

WEAVER HILLS—3 MILES..................

CHEDDLETON & THE CALDON CANAL—

2, 2 1/2, 4 1/2, AND 7MILES..................

FROGHALL AND CALDON CANAL—5 & 6 MILES..................

ALTON AND THE CHURNET VALLEY—5 MILES..................

ALTON AND BRADLEY IN THE MOORS—8 MILES..................

OAKAMOOR AND FARLEY—5 MILES..................

OAKAMOOR AND WHISTON—8 MILES..................

DIMMINGS DALE AND OUSAL DALE—2 1/2 & 3 1/2 MILES..................

HAWKSMOOR—4 MILES..................

THE MANIFOLD VALLEY—

ECTON AND THE MANIFOLD VALLEY—4 MILES (2 WALKS)..................

WETTON AND THOR'S CAVE—4 1/2 MILES..................

HAMPS VALLEY AND MUSDEN WOOD—6 & 8 MILES..................

WATERHOUSES AND CAULDON—2 MILES..................

DOVEDALE AREA—

HARTINGTON, BERESFORD DALE & BIGGIN DALE—5 MILES..................

ALSTONEFIELD AND MILLDALE—4 MILES..................

ILAM AND DOVEDALE—7 MILES..................

THE JOHN MERRILL WALK BADGE

Complete six walks in this book and get the above special embroidered badge and signed certificate. Badges are black cloth with lettering and man in four colours and measure 3 1/2 dia.

BADGE ORDER FORM

Date walk completed..

....

NAME ....

ADDRESS ....

....

Price: £3.00 each including postage, VAT and signed completion certificate.
Amount enclosed (Payable to *Happy Walking International Ltd*) ..

From: Happy Walking International Ltd.,
Unit 1, Molyneux Business Park, Darley Dale,
Matlock, Derbyshire. DE4 2HJ
✆ /**Fax** (01629) - 735911

********** *YOU MAY PHOTOCOPY THIS FORM* ***********

"I'VE DONE A JOHN MERRILL WALK" T SHIRT

- Green with white lettering and walking man logo.

Send £7.50 to *Happy Walking International Ltd.*, stating size required.

John Merrill's "Happy Walking!" Cap - £3.50

Happy Walking Button Badge - 50p inc p & p.

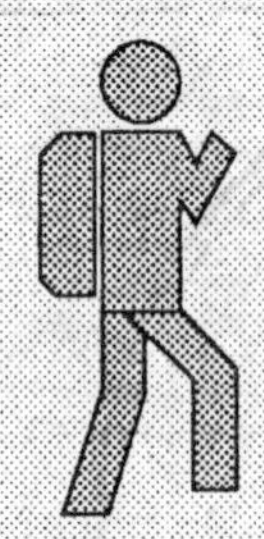

Remember and observe the Country Code

Enjoy the countryside and respect its life and work.

Guard against all risk of fire.

Fasten all gates.

Keep your dogs under close control.

Keep to public paths across farmland.

Use gates and stiles to cross fences, hedges and walls.

Leave livestock, crops and machinery alone.

Take your litter home - pack it in; pack it out.

Help to keep all water clean.

Protect wildlife, plants and trees.

Take special care on country roads

Make no unnecessary noise.

THE LITTLE JOHN CHALLENGE WALK
YORKSHIRE DALES CHALLENGE WALK
NORTH YORKSHIRE MOORS CHALLENGE WALK
LAKELAND CHALLENGE WALK
THE RUTLAND WATER CHALLENGE WALK
MALVERN HILLS CHALLENGE WALK
THE SALTER'S WAY
THE SNOWDON CHALLENGE
CHARNWOOD FOREST CHALLENGE WALK
THREE COUNTIES CHALLENGE WALK (Peak District).
CAL-DER-WENT WALK by Geoffrey Carr,
THE QUANTOCK WAY
BELVOIR WITCHES CHALLENGE WALK
THE CARNEDDAU CHALLENGE WALK

INSTRUCTION & RECORD -
HIKE TO BE FIT.....STROLLING WITH JOHN
THE JOHN MERRILL WALK RECORD BOOK

MULTIPLE DAY WALKS -
THE RIVERS'S WAY
PEAK DISTRICT: HIGH LEVEL ROUTE
PEAK DISTRICT MARATHONS
THE LIMEY WAY
THE PEAKLAND WAY
COMPO'S WAY by Alan Hiley

COAST WALKS & NATIONAL TRAILS -
ISLE OF WIGHT COAST PATH
PEMBROKESHIRE COAST PATH
THE CLEVELAND WAY
WALKING ANGELSEY'S COASTLINE.

CYCLING *Compiled by Arnold Robinson.*
CYCLING AROUND THE NORTH YORK MOORS .
CYCLING AROUND MATLOCK.
CYCLING AROUND LEICES & RUTLAND.
CYCLING AROUND CASTLETON & the Hope Valley.
CYCLING AROUND CHESTERFIELD.
CYCLING IN THE YORKSHIRE WOLDS
CYCLING AROUND BUXTON.
CYCLING AROUND LINCOLNSHIRE.

PEAK DISTRICT HISTORICAL GUIDES -
A to Z GUIDE OF THE PEAK DISTRICT
DERBYSHIRE INNS - an A to Z guide
HALLS AND CASTLES OF THE PEAK DISTRICT & DERBYSHIRE
TOURING THE PEAK DISTRICT & DERBYSHIRE BY CAR
DERBYSHIRE FOLKLORE
PUNISHMENT IN DERBYSHIRE
CUSTOMS OF THE PEAK DISTRICT & DERBYSHIRE
WINSTER - a souvenir guide
ARKWRIGHT OF CROMFORD
LEGENDS OF DERBYSHIRE
DERBYSHIRE FACTS & RECORDS
TALES FROM THE MINES by Geoffrey Carr
PEAK DISTRICT PLACE NAMES by Martin Spray

JOHN MERRILL'S MAJOR WALKS -
TURN RIGHT AT LAND'S END
WITH MUSTARD ON MY BACK
TURN RIGHT AT DEATH VALLEY
EMERALD COAST WALK

SKETCH BOOKS -
SKETCHES OF THE PEAK DISTRICT

COLOUR BOOK:-
THE PEAK DISTRICT......something to remember her by.

OVERSEAS GUIDES -
HIKING IN NEW MEXICO - Vol I - The Sandia and Manzano Mountains.
Vol 2 - Hiking "Billy the Kid" Country. Vol 4 - N.W. area - " Hiking Indian Country."
"WALKING IN DRACULA COUNTRY" - Romania.

VISITOR GUIDES - *MATLOCK . BAKEWELL. ASHBOURNE.*